Connecting Hearts
Connecting Generations

Muhammad Osimi

To order additional copies of this book, contact:
Xlibris
844-714-8691
www.Xlibris.com
Orders@Xlibris.com

ISBN:	Softcover	979-8-3694-3781-0
	Hardcover	979-8-3694-3783-4
	EBook	979-8-3694-3782-7

Library of Congress Control Number: 2024927435

Print information available on the last page

Rev. date: 12/26/2024

"In the future, interaction and mutual influence of cultures will continue to intensify. And concurrently, a synthesis of cultures will also begin to take place, which will serve the noble cause of bringing nations together."

Muhammad Osimi

Dear Reader,

This volume comprises essential interviews of our late father, Tajik Scholar, philosopher, historian, intellectual and humanist, President of the Tajik Academy of Sciences, Jawaharlal Nehru Award winner, and a founder of "Payvand"("Unity"-an international organization of cultural relations between the Tajiks and compatriots and co-linguists around the world), the President of UNESCO's International Association of the Study of Civilization and Cultures of Central Asia, Academician Muhammad Osimi from 1990 to his last interview in 1996. It was the period of a crisis in Tajik history marking the transition of the nation to democratic dispensation. Since then, the nation has taken significant strides on the path of democracy and progress.

Contemporary history of Tajikistan has shown that the experience and vision of our late father as reflected in these interviews have great relevance for all times. We have to understand and put to practice the imperative of social cohesion and connectivity stressed by Osimi.

The book you are holding is the result of the hard work, perseverance and dedication to our dear father by our late mother, Monand Osimi.

We would like to pay tribute to the memory of our mother, who was the real guiding force behind our father. She passed away the same month as his death fourteen years later.

Our mother was a typical traditional Tajik woman who had imbibed the values and the discipline set forth by Khujand's society and traditions over long years of its existence. She was well aware of Tajik history and had excellent grasp of Tajik literature necessary to illuminate any formal or informal function.

She was a model of courage, perseverance and dedication to the cause of humanitarianism. Our mother was the ideal Tajik mother, daughter, wife, and grandmother. As she was bestowed with wisdom and maturity, throughout their fifty five years of marriage, our father always placed the highest value in her opinion. She was always the first listener and the first critic of his speeches. Because of this exchange, our parents often joked that our mother completed her education from the great university of our father. She was a true companion to him.

It is extremely painful to think of the sadness and grief that overtook our mother when our father's life was taken by the bullet of an assassin. A woman of great fortitude, our mother bore the tragedy and separation from her life partner by resigning to her destiny. However, instead of succumbing to her grief, she dedicated herself to continuing the work of our father with strength and grace. She has published many of his works, organized his archives and photographs and has given many interviews about him.

She lives in our memory, and her character serves as an exemplary model that we, her children, will continue to cherish and preserve.

The original version of this volume was published in Tajik under the direction of Yuldashev Nabijon by Khoorasan Publication in Khujand in 2006. This volume was also published in Farsi under the supervision of the late Professor Abdulqadir Maniyazov . Shahnoz Benazir (Osimi's granddaughter-in-law), created the Farsi transcript.

Professor Kashinath Pandita, the steadfast Indian scholar, friend of Tajiks and a dear friend of Osimi and his family, became inspired by this book and volunteered to translate it into English to pay homage to his late friend. This volume also contains an article written by him in which he shares with us his deep memories of Osimi.

Dr. Pandita holds a PhD from Tehran University and is a professor at the Centre of Central Asian Studies at Kashmir University. Dr. Pandita has been actively collaborating with Central Asian scholars as well as traveling to the region. His work has culminated in the publication of a travelogue entitled *My Tajik Friends*, which has won him the Soviet Nehru Award in 1987 and has since been translated into Russian. He is an honorary member of Payvand.

After the enemies of humanity put a brutal end to the life of our father in 1996, this Indian friend of Tajiks, found us, the children, the bereaved members of Osimi's family, and gave us much needed moral and spiritual support to bear the tragedy. His role in reviving the spirit of our family serves as a symbol of deep devotion to human relationships and universal bonds that transcend all physical and notional barriers.

On behalf of the members of Osimi family, we express our most sincere and deep appreciation to this rare and selfless Indian scholar and friend of Tajiks.

We would like to thank Dr. Tej Nath Dhar, former Professor of English and Dean of the Faculty of Arts, Asmara University, Asmara, Eritrea, for editing the English text.

Taking this opportunity we express our gratitude to all our father's and our family friends.

With the best wishes and profound thankfulness,
The family of Muhammad Osimi.

CONTENTS

FOREWORD

PAYVAND — The Icon

The second half of the 1980s, particularly the period after Tajikistan attained complete national independence in 1991, created opportunities of establishing contact with our compatriots, whom the cataclysms of time and history of near and distant past, had sent on forced dispersal to different corners of the world. With the intention of knowing them fully and establishing rapport with them, the international organization of cultural relations between the Tajiks and compatriots and co-linguists outside the country established *Payvand* in October 1989. It was popularly known as *Anjuman-e-Payvand'*

Prominent among the founders of the *Anjuman-e-Payvand* was the renowned scholar, the leading cultural figure and the outstanding Tajik personality in the service of the government and civil society, Muhammad Saifudinovich Osimi. He had the distinction of becoming the first elected President of this organization.

Muhammad Osimi, a distinguished academician had already gained a rich experience of running such a prestigious organization. He had held the important positions of Chancellor of Polytechnic University (now re-named Osimi Tajik Technical University), Minister for Education (Teaching and Training), Secretary of Central Committee of Communist Party and Deputy Chief of the Council of Ministers of Tajikistan. His long stint as President of the Academy of Sciences, Tajikistan had earned him a fund of administrative skills, which stood him in good stead in running the affairs of *Payvand*. Even before the establishment of this organization, he had been fully conscious of the need for establishing a creative relationship between the Tajik scholars, writers, thinkers and cultural personalities and their counterparts in foreign countries, he, in fact, considered it his biggest and the most important duty. The aims and aspirations of the Payvand organization demanded that Osimi give a wider and more vibrant dimension to his managerial potential.

Osimi was cultured and knowledgeable and gifted with the higher quality of virtue. He could cultivate close friendship with people bestowed with excellence and cultural richness.

Osimi had developed close collaborative relations with his compatriots and co-linguists. He ardently desired that Farsi speaking peoples develop close mutual contacts so that exchange of their scholarly works would become a reality. He traveled to many parts of the world for participating in conferences and seminars. In the process he added new names to his long list of friends and well-wishers.

Keeping in mind his mission and his versatility, the election of Osimi to the office of the President of *Payvand* was actually an apt and befitting act to confer an icon on the organization, the icon of friendship and connectivity. This was why within a short period of time under his chairmanship, the *Payvand* graduated to an institution of profound influence and credibility. Soon it attracted renowned personalities of erudition, culture and of Farsi scholarship to its assemblies.

A conspicuous achievement of Payvand under Osimi's stewardship was the first conclave of the Tajik scholars, compatriots and co-linguists, within and outside the country, in Dushanbe on September 9, 1992 in connection with celebrating the first anniversary of Tajikistan's independence. That was a time when the country was passing through a bloody civil war and internal strife, and one needed extraordinary courage to visit Tajikistan. However, out of four hundred persons invited from all over the world, nearly 370 guests from 19 countries did make it. Evidently, their sentiment of pride in seeing a newly independent Tajikistan with their own eyes outstripped the dangers and perils involved in visiting their ancestral land.

The participants in the conclave, our compatriots who had placed their foot on the soil of their ancestors after a long absence, were infused with deep love for their native land. They passionately desired that a conclave of the Tajiks be held every year to commemorate the Independence Day of Tajikistan.

Precisely a year later, in the month of September 1993, the second conclave of the Tajiks was held in Dushanbe. This time an independent international organization by the name of Association of World Tajik-Farsi Speaking Scholars was incepted. The conclave endorsed the statutes and structure of the organization.

In this conclave, the President of the Republic of Tajikistan, Imamali Shariefovich Rahmanov,[1] who also happened to be the President of the Supreme Council of the Republic at that time, was elected President of the Association of World Tajik-Farsi Language Scholars by the body of participants of the conclave. In his capacity as the Chairman of *Payvand*, Prof Osimi undertook to perform the duties of the Chief of the Executive Body and to look after the preparations for the third Conclave to be held in September 1996. How tragic that fate prevented him from participating in that conference!

Scholars, literary luminaries, connoisseurs of art and literature, thankful people of Tajikistan and the guests from abroad who flock to Payvand, all express their great appreciation and gratitude to Professor Osimi. They call Osimi a man with pristine disposition, an astute scholar and a noble son of Tajik nation. Recognizing the value of the services of Osimi to his nation, the President of the Republic of Tajikistan and the President of the World Association of Tajik-Farsi Speaking Scholars, President Imamali Shariefovich Rahmanov said," As the founder of this Association and the coordinator of fraternal relations with the compatriots abroad, Professor Muhammad Osimi has rendered befitting service to the development and expansion of knowledge and culture in our motherland. This celebrated scholar has left behind him a valuable record of writings in the history of philosophy, especially scientific and philosophical transactions of eastern people, and history of science and literature. Owing to his efforts several international seminars and symposia of high academic level pertaining to the history and civilization of the people of the people of the East were organized in Tajikistan."

This year 2006 we celebrate the 15th year of Tajikistan's independence together with 2700th year of the founding of the ancient city of Kulab and the anniversary of Aryan Civilization. Simultaneously, we organized the sixth annual conference of the World Association of Tajik-Farsi Language Scholars.

During the preceding decade, our nation succeeded in promoting national consensus (among political groups), and an atmosphere of peace. We have landed in an era of creativity and continuity and we have achieved big successes in almost all walks of life. The activities of *Payvand* also witnessed noticeable movement forward. In all these achievements, the contribution of our immortal guide Professor Osimi is explicit. In our nation's march to future prosperity, he walks step by step by our side.

Osimi's life partner Madam Manandkhon, and his children have compiled this work as a collection of the speeches and statements of this great son of the soil to the media. They have printed the volume and gifted it to this Association. We shall be spending some time in the sweet company of late Professor Osimi while we run through the pages of this publication.

Abdul Qadir Maniyazov,
President Executive Committee *Payvand*.

TRANSLATOR'S INTRODUCTION

Observers of Soviet history were disposed to over-emphasise the importance of the era of Perestroika and Glasnost of 1980s. President Gorbachev had tried to take the time by forelock. His speeches and statements, though dealing with generalities, were sufficiently indicative of rumblings in the CPSU and Soviet society. The lurking urge for a change could not be suppressed for too long. Political pundits have extensively debated the emergence of the new phenomenon but its impact on Central Asian society and the reaction thereto needs to be recapitulated.

Tajik watchers, dealing with contemporary history, have tried to explain the reasons why this one time "Soviet underbelly" was sucked into the vortex of a civil war soon after the declaration of independence in 1991. Of the five Central Asian and two Trans-Caspian states of the erstwhile Soviet Central Asia, Tajikistan was economically the weakest state. With barely 4 percent of land available for agricultural purposes, and industry almost non-existent, Tajikistan was faced with the acute problem of a surplus of manpower leading to high youth unemployment. Would Perestroika and Glasnost bring any relief and hope to this restive populace? It was a moot question.

Tajikistan was the only state of Central Asia where, soon after the declaration of independence, a civil war broke out. Why did the fratricide take place only in Tajikistan? Historians will focus attention on that question. There could be many reasons.

To the south of Tajikistan lies Afghanistan, a state drawn into fierce political rivalry between the two super powers, each buttressed by respective allies and camp followers in the region. Inducting Soviet troops into Afghanistan for active intervention in 1979, was one among many foolhardy acts of the Soviet regime. It had to pay a heavy price for its intransigence. Apart from repercussions for the Soviet state, armed intervention in Afghanistan had significant impact on international politics and geopolitical strategies. Afghanistan, a land that had remained consigned to oblivion for a long period, suddenly emerged on the world political scene. Events shaping there gave a new direction to geopolitical strategies in Asia and the world. Something very consequential was happening on the southern border of Tajikistan in which big powers evinced keen interest. How could the tiny state of Tajikistan remain unaffected by all this?

Soviet incursion into Afghanistan opened the road for free flow of arms, ammunition, fundamentalist ideology, volunteers, suicide squads (*fidayeen*) and the heartless intelligence operatives from all those places and people who would venture to fish in troubled waters. Neighbouring states apart, an interventionist role was played by radical groups and organizations drawing inspirations from Sunni-Wahhabi school of thought and operating on lands not far away from Tajikistan.

Much earlier than the days of launching Perestroika and Glasnost, the Soviet administration had detected the presence of rabid Wahhabi missionaries active in remote and rather less accessible parts of

Tajikistan. The mosque is a safe haven where the youth can be indoctrinated with religious extremist philosophy. With the declaration of independence in 1991 and recognition by the world community, the sovereign state of Tajikistan began exercising her domestic and foreign policy as she thought best in her national interests. She announced that she would be friendly to all and hostile to none. However, some neighbouring Islamic states, driven by the erratic impression that following the implosion of the Soviet Union, a vacuum had appeared in Central Asian states, hastened to fill it by offering them strong prescription of Islamic revivalism. Ethnic and linguistic cards were also put on the table and old Turkic-Iranian ethnic divide was played up in the hope of finding depth in the lands and the peoples of Turkestan. This myopic vision ultimately exposed their ignorance of the changes, which three-quarters of a century-long Soviet rule had brought to the traditional Central Asia. A witty Tajik observer remarked, "When we realised that their grip was coming close to strangle us, we cut off their hand and hurled it away".

The rise of Taliban in Afghanistan and the resultant ethnic war between the predominantly Pushtuns of Southern Afghanistan on one side and Tajik-Uzbek combination of Northern Afghanistan on the other, made the Afghan – Tajik border immensely volatile. Unfortunately, the ethnic and sectarian virus let loose by the mujahideen under their new avatar of the Taliban in the aftermath of massive American arms supplies and rigorous indoctrination in Pakistani seminaries, seriously shook The Tajik civil society.

Tajikistan slipped into disastrous civil war. Polarisation took place along ethnic, ideological and even sectarian lines. Radicals and conformists took on liberals. The capital city of Dushanbe became a virtual battlefield for the conflicting and antagonistic groups. Portable arms flowed freely, obviously smuggled clandestinely across the Tajik-Afghan border or looted from erstwhile Soviet arsenals, and shootouts between the rival groups became a daily routine. Law and order broke down, the economy collapsed and the civil society was dragged to the verge of disintegration. The once orderly and disciplined Tajik nation, proud of its history and rich civilization was threatened with extinction.

Yet another dreary aspect of the fratricidal war was that hundreds of thousands of Tajiks fled their homes, crossed over to the Afghan side of the border and took shelter in refugee camps. Many of them received succour from their relatives, friends and acquaintances among ethnic Tajik Afghans. They left their homes partly owing to the fear of rampaging armed gangsters and partly because of ideological divide. At the same time, anti-social elements indulged in churning rumours and canards in order to stoke the flames of conflict and contradiction. This depressing scenario spoke of a critical phase through which Tajikistan was passing.

Tajik leadership was as much alarmed by this depressing situation as the ordinary citizens. Shortage of food supplies and other essential consumer goods in the capital city owing to insecurity of transit and transportation routs could lead to a spree of loot and arson particularly when the law-enforcing agency remained paralysed. In an utterly confusing political scenario, people shifted allegiance from one group to another only to reverse it sooner than later. One could say that Tajik personality and identity were in the throes of distortion.

Earlier, during the time of the success of the Bolshevik revolution and Tajikistan becoming a federated unit of the Soviet Union, many Tajiks did not reconcile to the communist order. With the liquidation of Basmachis, these dissidents left Tajikistan for a foreign land and ultimately settled down there braving with fortitude many hardships and hazards of life among aliens. A good number of these émigrés settled down in the city of New York in USA.

Obviously, these Tajik émigrés yearned for the land of their birth and the land where lay the ashes of their forebears. In international parlance they were asylum seekers against ideological persecution at home. Under Soviet regime their return to their native land was disallowed because those who sought asylum were labelled as enemies of the State and fifth columnists. It was next to impossible for them to establish any contact with their kith and kin back home leave aside meeting with them in person. Soviet Union was extremely miserly in permitting its nationals to visit their kith and kin in a western country. Such was the impact of the iron curtain behind which the Soviet Union stood.

The ruling structure in Tajikistan did nurse the hope that Perestroika and Glasnost would partially address the issue of Tajik émigrés desirous of reunion with their compatriots. If this long-standing deprivation was to be removed, then a viable and effective mechanism had to be in place. Careful analysis revealed that this sensitive issue could not be tackled by raw hands and without an element of deep and dispassionate humanism. We shall have more to say on this subject later on in this introduction.

When Tajikistan declared her independence, the question of return of the natives, primarily the Tajik refugees in Afghanistan, was one that had to be addressed urgently. The refugees needed convincing assurance that no vendetta would be unleashed against them and that they would be able to resume their normal life back home without interference and intimidation. As long as the fratricidal war was going on, this objective was very difficult to achieve. It meant that conditions had to be created in which concerned parties would be goaded into abandoning their selfish aggrandisement and give the first priority to national interests.

Another question, which worried Tajik authorities, was that of not too sympathetic an attitude by some of the neighbouring governments and their institutions towards the beleaguered and landlocked country. How ironic if they did not have the vision that an endangered Tajikistan would be more a cause of concern than relief to them. The threat of ethnic, territorial and other bilateral and multilateral disputes could lead to a disastrous conflict opening the floodgates of external intervention. This was one of the main reasons why Moscow hurried to forge a cooperation of sorts among its former confederates, under the new name of Commonwealth of Independent States (CIS).

Tajikistan needed visionary leadership to handle the delicate situation. Real ground work lay at home. An atmosphere of congeniality had to be created. The nation's mind had to be prepared for a thrust forward. New paths had to be broken and new ideas introduced. The Tajik nation had to be pulled out of the shock and trauma it had suffered. The meaning of independence, which had hitherto remained elusive, had to be translated into practice. Thus the work of building new Tajikistan encompassed all aspects, political, economic, social, constitutional, administrative, and financial. It was a testing time, indeed.

Fortunately, Tajikistan created leadership that could rise to the occasion. With patience, astute statesmanship and with great political sagacity, Tajik lawmakers and administrators worked out rapprochement with the dissenting fraction. The policy of give and take worked well and a coalition government enfolding various shades of opinion was formed. An understanding was struck with the opposition in 1996 and national interests were safeguarded. Tajikistan could pull itself out of critical and disheartening conditions of early days of independence. Law and order steadily returned to the strife-torn state. Administration became functional. The semblance of peace prompted foreign investors to invest in vital industries of the country. Trade and commerce became vibrant and commercial routes were opened. Internal security came to be established and life began to return to normal in towns and rural areas. Government institutions resumed their routine work.

With conditions stabilising at home, Tajikistan began to look for her identity. From among five nations of Central Asia, she was the only one of Aryan stock. Her history, civilization, language, literature and life style were an integral part of the Irano-Aryan and not Turko-Mongolian civilization. Ever since the dismemberment of Samanian kingdom in about 1000 A.D. Tajiks felt that they were lost to the world in a sense. Theirs was a sad story indeed and history had hardly been sympathetic to them. Subjugated by Arabs in 7/8th century A.D., uprooted by fanatical Ghaznavids in early 10th century, crushed by Mongol hordes in 13th century, over run by ruthless nomadic warlords, chieftains and satraps for another two centuries, suppressed by the autocratic and tyrannical Khans of Bukhara in 18th/19th century, conquered by the imperial Czarists in 19th century and Sovietized in the first few decades of 20th century, it was only in the closing decade of the 20th century that the Tajiks began to breath an air of freedom and self rule after remaining in oblivion for nearly a millennium.

Therefore they were justified in projecting their identity and underlining their individuality. Installation of the stately statue of the great Samanid ruler, Ismael Samani, in a grand and imposing ceremony in 1998 in the Maidan Dosti of the capital city Dushanbe, was an important step towards the realization of that dream. It lent cohesion, unity and national integrity to the newfound Tajik nation. The symbol had historical and cultural import.

As we are talking of national integrity and identity, it is sad to say that during the Soviet era, a great injustice was done to them by detaching two fabulous cities of Central Asia, also the traditional centres of Tajik history and civilization, namely Samarkand and Bukhara, from the newly carved Soviet Central Asian Republic of Tajikistan. As a result of cartographic engineering undertaken by the demarcation committee under the chairmanship of Stalin, the two cities became part of Uzbekistan. Tajiks have not reconciled to this arbitrary and irrational decision, much less the predominantly Tajik population of the twin cities. It has remained an irritant in good relations between the two neighbouring states. The Tajiks have always considered it a serious loss of their civilization fund and thus a blow to their identity. Yet, the reality on the ground is that this historic and rather unjust decision may not be reversed. Therefore the impact the loss had to be softened and considerably reduced by resorting to the logic of history. Tajikistan needed farsighted statesmanship to handle this volatile issue. If the two peoples were to remain at loggerheads, it would adversely affect their economy and development. Areas of goodwill had to be identified and expanded. A new chapter had to be opened in the history of bilateral relations not only with Uzbekistan but also with all the erstwhile Central Asian republics of the Soviet Union.

Notwithstanding a long period of cataclysms, Tajiks clung to symbols of their antiquated civilization while adapting to new and healthy trends brought by Islamic faith through missionaries and administrative mechanisms. In the process, they did somehow preserve the pre-Islamic traditions generally attributed to Zoroastrian period. It essentially manifested in the formation of a tolerant attitude towards other faiths whose adherents enjoyed social freedom more than anywhere else in the Islamised world. There were the

Jews, the Shia', the Ismailis the Zoroastrians, non-conformists and others. There were still pockets in the mountains of Badakhshan where people held on to ancient Zoroastrian traditions. There were the Sogdians in the Zarafshan Valley who were rightfully proud of their fabulous contribution to the Tajik and Central Asian civilization. There were the Kulabis who had contributed to the Islamic civilization of Central Asia, the Sufi traditions and the philosophy of human brotherhood. There were the Khujandis who had borne the brunt of many fierce onslaughts of invaders and foreign warlords. This colourful mosaic of society lived in harmony and over the centuries silently contributed to the enrichment of Central Asian civilization.

Independence also brought many responsibilities. For Tajik people and their leadership, it was a moment of trial. They were at a crucial stage of their history. Would they come out of a thousand year old oblivion and march shoulder to shoulder with living and moving nations of the world or would they go down and be lost for all times to come? The odds were many. A section of people radicalised by intransigent politicians wanted to rent the social fabric of Tajik society asunder. It conspired to put a liberal, progressive and forward-looking society into blinkers. This was against the spirit of tolerance and coexistence deeply cherished by the Tajik society.

Responsible Tajik leadership, demonstrating, courage, wisdom and statesmanship, steered the ship of the state through these storms. Step by step, the nation moved towards the recovery of its health. Tajikistan became a member of the comity of nations and was granted membership of the United Nations. She became a signatory to UN Protocols and Charters that enjoin upon members to preserve and promote cordial and friendly relations with all nations. She committed herself to regional and international peace and progress. Dignitaries from developed western countries and developing countries began visiting Tajikistan and Tajik leaders reciprocated good will and business visits. Tajikistan's identity as an ancient nation with rich past and colourful civilization began crystallising. As her profile grew, foreign investment prospects brightened. Multinationals began to open their branches in Tajikistan, which was bound to create job opportunities and economic revival. The educational system began to be reformed and learning English became a fashion with the youngsters. Tajikistan was on a move toward a new phase of modernisation.

Yet notwithstanding a radical change into which the country landed, Tajik leadership took care not to loose what had been achieved during seventy-five years of Soviet rule. Russian continued to be the official language though Tajik in Cyrillic script also continued to enjoy the respect shown to it. Tajik language and literature received new impetus when cultural exchanges between Tajikistan and Iran became more and more frequent. Tajik language spoken and written today has a fairly large sprinkling of current terminology that is in use in Iran and one who has been a close watcher of Tajik cultural trends, has no difficulty in noticing the enrichment of Tajik language from what it was say twenty years ago.

Another aspect worth mentioning is that tens of thousands of Tajiks who migrated to foreign countries including parts of the Russian Federation, the US, Saudi Arabia and the European countries for one reason or the other, are now evincing keener and keener interest in the affairs of their native land and her people. Previously, they were scared even to disclose their identity and address as they were looked upon as the agents and spies of the enemy – imperialism. How would the independent Tajikistan deal with this important issue?

Part II

At this point of time of her history there appeared on the stage a noble son of Tajikistan who was greater than his size. Saifu'd-Din Muhammad Osimi, a scholar, thinker, scientist and above all the icon of Tajik culture was in the forefront of caretakers of the beleaguered nation. Like Maulana Jalau'd-Din Rumi, the great philosopher, poet and intellectual from Balkh, who had infused the beleaguered Muslim communities with urge and courage to rise from the ashes of Mongol depredations, Osimi sent a loud and clear massage to his Tajik compatriots at home and abroad that harked them back to their days of glory, grandeur and greatness. A soldier, scholar, erudite, administrator, leader and a social scientist of exemplary dedication, Osimi was literally a man of multi-dimensional personality whom the Tajiks of our days considered the icon of their culture, history and civilization. Osimi had travelled extensively and had a vast circle of friends all over the globe who looked at him as the ideal representative of the fabulous Central Asian civilization. In the neighbouring Asian countries, which had age-old relations with Tajikistan, like Iran, India, Pakistan, Afghanistan and Saudi Arabia, Osimi was taken as Tajikistan's unofficial ambassador. He commanded popularity and respect in these countries and also on international level so much so that the UNESCO felt happy to make him the Chairman of the Committee for writing 5-volume History of Central Asia. With the passage of time, he had grown into an institution.

Osimi was the inheritor of modern Tajik cultural fund and nationalism, the foundation of which had been laid by eminent Tajiks like Abul Qasim Lahuti, Sadru'd-Din Aini, Torsun Zadeh, Babajan Ghafarov and others. In his turn, he was not only the conduit linking the traditional and the modern but was also the mentor of a new generation of Tajik : intellectual who would soon be called upon to carry the responsibility of guiding the nation with poise and dignity and to reach a place of honour and respect among the comity of nations. Even a cursory interaction with him showed that he could think beyond his times, his people and his land. He was gifted with world vision and hence was a citizen of the world in real sense of the term.

Taking cue from the stated objectives of Gorbachev's reformative philosophy enshrined in the concept of Perestroika and Glasnost, Osimi nicely dovetailed it with the need for the Tajik nation to initiate cultural consolidation. Focusing on the basics of Tajikistan's identity as an instrument to forge national integrity, and supported by the ruling authority of the day, Osimi conceived, proposed and formulated the important organization now called Payvand (literally meaning The Link), that was to become the most effective instrument of bringing Tajiks all over the world together on one platform for deliberating on the present situation and future course of the independent nation of the Tajiks.

Osimi knew his people and their problems. Osimi knew the world around and the trends that were shaping in it. He could not step back and remain inactive. Other republics of Central Asia were also engaged in search of their identity after the Perestroika era set in. Osimi, too, had his agenda for his nation. Obviously, he had to make a small beginning. Funds were not easy to come. He could not go beyond his sheet. Perestroika was fine, but then the communist steel frame was still there. It had to be reckoned with. Speaking to the correspondent of *Tajikistan* in Dushanbe in February 1990, Professor Osimi explained the purpose of setting up the Association of Payvand (*Anjuman-e Payvand*) as this:

> "I have often traveled to foreign countries including those in the East in connection with
> official assignments. I often cherished to reach my compatriots abroad. I came to know of their
> despair and deprivations. I found that they did not broach animus towards their native land or

towards the Soviet Union. Contrarily, they desired that good and solid relations were established between us. They wanted to have more information about the life in Tajikistan. I have visited the localities of the people from Samarkand, Bukhara, Khujand and Ferghana in cities like Isfahan, Baghdad, Bombay and Delhi. Most of them are fairly prosperous. They do not suffer from scarcity of anything. But separation from their native land gives them pangs of suffering. I have often heard them utter:

Atre kafan ze khak-e watan kardam arzu
Wa hasrata kih mi baram in arzu be khak

Long did I cherish to anoint my coffin with the dust of my native land?
Oh Despair! I carry the wish with me down into my grave

How nice if a heart reaches a heart, a friend reaches a friend and a generation reaches a generation? How nice that after long and painful separation, there is reunion and rejoicing."

But before *Payvand* could embark on its ambitious mission, Tajikistan was sucked into the disastrous civil war. *Payvand*, like all institutions of civil society, was faced with a new situation that threatened the very fabric of nation's cohesion. The government had to prioritize its options. All institutions were geared up to face the delicate situation and Osimi sat down to ruminate coolly over all that he and his organizations were faced with. His organization was above party politics, above ideological divide and above regional affiliations. His raw material was the Tajiks, in all their simplicity and innocence, and bandaged in all their historical and cultural legacies. In that sense, Osimi had much heavy a burden to carry and much weighty a responsibility to shoulder.

Was the *Payvand* to temporarily shift its goal posts or was it to add another dimension to its objectives and aims, namely the politics of reconciliation? Surely, that option became a priority with him. He did not mince words when questions in that context were put to him. And he was right. *Payvand* had to play the role of an effective instrument in restoring confidence among the people and harking them back to their great humanistic traditions. More than that, *Payvand* had to become a credible instrument for joining hearts. Tajik émigrés, who had been forced to leave their birthplace for one or the other reason, were an asset to the nascent Tajik Republic. The home chapter desperately needed their cooperation and collaboration in rebuilding Tajikistan. They could contribute in many ways. But the question was of allaying their fears and suspicions. After all for more than half a century, they had been treated very poorly. Their loyalty was suspected and their intentions were questioned. They were treated more like spies and agents than honourable citizens. Even contacting them indirectly was a culpable crime under Soviet rigorous dispensation. They had a grouse against their own compatriots back home who had, at times, behaved more loyal than the king.

The task before Osimi was forbidding. He could anticipate the quantum of resentment he would have to face from the Tajiks abroad if he decided to proceed on a meaningful mission to the US and other western countries. The Tajik government did not find a man more capable than Osimi to undertake this onerous mission. The veteran nationalist, the adroit humanist and the skillful negotiator demonstrated extraordinary self-confidence to undertake the mission, come what may. Tajikistan needed people dedicated to rebuilding the devastated country. Osimi took with him a small team and proceeded to the US on his first trip to seek, contact and engage in a dialogue with his long estranged compatriots. He succeeded, as you will discover while going through the pages of this book.

The times were hard for *Payvand* and its founder and President, Muhamamd Osimi. A wave of hatred had swayed some sections of Tajik society. They spoke the language of communalists and those who advocated sectarianism. Among the émigrés was a large number of Tajik Jews settled mostly in New York and Israel. The Sunni-Wahhabis, as we know, bore animus against them. Iran's Islamic revolutionaries made no objections about that. And many Wahhabis continued to receive inspiration from them. This was apart from a fierce hate campaign unleashed on ethnic and regional count. How Osimi reacted to it is a unique example of the broad vision of a statesman of his stature. He dealt with these issues in his interviews candidly. He emphasized that the only option before the nation was to rise above sectarianism, parochialism and regionalism. He emphasized that no community in present day could either afford or decide to live in isolation or in a state of compartmentalization. He talked of universalism, of human fraternity and of historic bonds. He talked of Tajik-Farsi speaking peoples all over the world and he talked of their friends and colleagues in different walks of life in different parts of the globe.

For reasons hinted elsewhere in the introduction, Tajiks and Uzbeks are somewhat estranged people today. For sure there is a communication gap between them. But at the same time, we are aware that hundreds of thousands of Uzbeks are living in Tajikistan and the vice versa. How can these people, who are bound by historical, geographical, social and cultural ties over a long period of time, continue to behave as adversaries? Osimi has very ably dealt with this subject in the course of his interviews to the correspondents and I do not find it necessary to repeat them here. But what is important is that Osimi has reacted with an eye on the future destiny of both the peoples. He is a lodestar not only for his compatriots but also for millions and millions of Central Asians who have sought habitation in states other than their own. The ultimate reality is that they have to live in peace and harmony with their local population.

A close study of the text of interviews will reveal that Osimi was using the instrument of *Payvand* to support and promote the foreign and domestic policy of his country. This certainly was not the primary purpose for which the organization had been incepted. But since the country had plunged into a very critical phase of her history, the *Payand* had the moral duty to make its input. There are various hints available in Osimi's interview that solidarity of the nation was the first and foremost task every Tajik was bound to undertake. A cultural organization of high national standing could not remain unconcerned about the impending threats to the solidarity and sovereignty of the state and the future of the people it represented. Osimi rightly visualised political, economic and social benefits likely to accrue to his country by widening the circle of friendly peoples and countries and maintaining steady links with them. He travelled far and wide; he interacted with people; he conveyed to them the message of peace and friendship; he developed personal rapport with outstanding personalities in all the countries he visited especially the neighbouring countries like Iran, Afghanistan, Pakistan, India and Turkey. Governors, ministers, Vice Chancellors, political havyweights and other dignitaries invited him to be their personal guest. He was the foremost Tajik known and respected in the erstwhile republics of Soviet Central Asia. He had a vast circle of friends and admirers in Moscow and at one point of time he was a running candidate for the prestigious position of President of the Soviet Academy of Sciences in Moscow.

During the most difficult times for Afghanistan in 1979, based on the initiative of Osimi, the Academy of Sciences of Afghanistan was founded. The purpose of this mission was to bring the scientists of the country together to work for the prosperity of Afghan nation.

For India, Osimi had very special regard, and called her the repository of Central Asian culture. He spoke with great pride and élan about the rich Indian libraries and archives housing very valuable Persian and Arabic manuscripts of eminent scholars of Central Asia and Iran. He fervently talked of great Mughal architectural monuments, which India has preserved and protected. Addressing a large gathering of students and teachers in Kashmir University in 1982, while he was in India in connection with the millennium celebration of celebrated Central Asian philosopher Abu Ali ibn Sina, Osimi told the audience that he was surprised to find Kashmiris using same names for the fruits as Tajiks did like *seb, anar, angur, tarboz, kharboz, hendwaneh, nakh, badam*, or trees like *chinar, bed, sarv, tut, shahtut, gulab*, etc. In great exultation Osimi told the audience at the end of his speech, "You are the crown on our head".

Osimi hailed from the suburbs of Khujand, a Central Asian town of mediaeval fame located along the eastern bank of Sir Darya. Khujand has been the field of and a witness to many great events of Central Asian history. The Mongol hordes and the Central Asian satraps fought many battles on the plains of Khujand to establish sway over the vast *Ma'vara'an'—nehr* or Transoxiana. Owing to brisk interaction among the people for trade and commerce and socialising activities, the people of Turkic and Aryan stocks became integrated into the broader Central Asian social milieu. Most of the people in historical Khujand were bi-lingual, because of cross-ethnic matrimonial alliances spread over many centuries, there sprang generations of mixed blood. Nevertheless, Tajik language and culture predominated in Khujand and the land produced many eminent men. Khujand can rightly boast of having given the Tajik nation an eminent son who illuminated the name of his people and his country. Osimi belongs to humanity and not only to his natives.

When Mahatma Gandhi was shot dead by an assailant, George Bernard Shaw said that the world had proved for the second time that it was too dangerous to be good. This remark of a great Scottish intellectual is also truer in the case of Osimi.

Kashinath Pandita
New Delhi
May 1, 2007

Source: Tajikistan, February,1990

Connecting Hearts, Connecting Generations

With the onset of the New Year, an important event shaped the political and social life of our Republic. The Association of Tajik Cultural Relations with Tajik Diaspora (Payvand) was incepted. The participants endorsed the statutes of the Association and elected its office bearers. On this occasion our correspondent interviewed with Muhammad Osimi, the President of the nascent Association, Academician of the Academy of Sciences of the Republic of Tajikistan and Associate Member of the USSR Academy of Sciences, about the aims and functions of Payvand.

———

Q: Revered Professor, first of all, will you kindly introduce Payvand Association to our distinguished readers.

Osimi: First let me make it clear that such organizations were incepted in most of the Republics of the Soviet Union long back. In other Republics these have been set up recently. Payvand is a peoples' organization, and works within the frame of the Constitution of Tajikistan and its Statutes. Soviet nationals, members of worker groups, people's associations and government institutions and also compatriots abroad and their organizations can take part in the activities of our Association out of their free will.
Payvand is a part of the larger concept of the country's reconstruction. It indicates many things: a change in the foreign policy of our government, sensitizing of new political thinking in our international relations, work towards peace and relaxation, closer interaction among human beings, cooperation and the unity and search of the Soviet people including the Tajiks for friendship and making many more friends.

Q: What was the need for creating an organization like this one?

A: I have to travel too often to foreign countries including those in the East in connection with official assignments. I often wanted to reach my compatriots living outside the country. I have known of the despair and deprivation of my compatriots. I have also found that they have no animus towards their native land or towards the Soviet Union. In fact, they also desired that solid relations be established between us. They wanted more information about life in Tajikistan. I have visited the localities of the people from Samarkand, Bukhara, Khujand and Ferghana in cities like Isfahan, Baghdad, Bombay and Dehli. Most of them are well off, but separation from their native land gives them pangs of suffering. I have often heard them say:

Atre kafan ze khak-e watan kardam arzu
Wa hasrata, kih mibaram in arzu be khak

Long did I cherish to anoint my coffin with the dust of my native land?
Oh Despair! I carry the wish with me into my grave

How nice if a heart reaches a heart, a friend reaches a friend and a generation reaches a generation? How nice that after long and painful separation, there is reunion and rejoicing. Our information is that there are millions of Farsi speaking peoples in the world, including the Tajiks. Most of them live in their native places. But the quirk of destiny forced others to become refugees. A large number of them are in Afghanistan, Pakistan, Hindustan and China.

Q: You attribute the migration of our compatriots to the quirk of destiny. Could you kindly elucidate that statement?

A: Yes, fate has dispersed them to places far away from their native land. Unfortunately, for long we chose to distance ourselves from them: we did not and we declined to establish bilateral relations with them, for we labeled them traitors and unpatriotic. We never tried to understand the pain in their hearts. We believed that one who leaves his native land is an anti-national, an alien country, and an enemy. We said that he had left and would return to his native land after undergoing a hundred privations. We said he was a spy.

Their departure was not a result of their own volition. In fact, history will show that the intelligentsia and the intellectuals of Transoxiana were oppressed and in order to escape the tyranny and control of the current rulers, were forced to choose the enlightened courts of Khorosan, Hindustan and some Arabic countries. One group of our compatriots migrated during the days of October Revolution, and the early years of a new governing dispensation for reasons known to all of us. Yet another group got stuck up at places outside the country during the scourge of World War II.

Let me draw your attention to one more point. When I say compatriot, I do not mean only the people of our (Tajik) community and our language. Owing to various incidents and exigencies of survival, Tajikistan had also become the native land for other ethnic groups such as the Germans and Tajik speaking Jews. They, too, had to migrate under because of adverse conditions. At present thousands of our compatriots are in Germany, Israel, United States, Austria, Sweden and several other countries. They have not totally cut off themselves from the soil of Tajikistan, but maintained contacts with it in whatever way they could. Some of our compatriots left with the purpose of joining their kith and kin. We cannot allow them to remain deprived of the love of their birthplace. We do not have the right to ignore them or their progeny.

Today, as a result of our efforts of reconstruction, this malaise of those days has been stamped out. Our changed conditions give a new respectability to our roots and our origins. We should not leave our former compatriots to their fate, but work to secure their links with the land of their ancestors and with the present and past of our country very strongly.

Q: Let us come to the basic purpose of our meeting: the fundamental duties of Payvand.

A: The aims and objectives of Payvand have been set forth in its constitution. Briefly, these are to apprise our compatriots abroad of our changed scenario of reconstruction, the broadening of democratic process, transparency and rejuvenation of various aspects of life of Soviet society; for example; extending support to those in Tajikistan who make efforts for preserving and strengthening cultural relations with our republic, contributing our share in coordinating the politics of reconstruction of our society and further strengthening friendship and positive collaboration between the Soviet Union and other countries. Among the important functions of Payvand are extending support to our compatriots for studying the history and culture of the people of our country, and creating conducive conditions for the progeny to learn Tajik language and literature.

Q: It is an exciting noble mission. Please tell us about the plans of Payvand to realize its stated goals?

A: We have several plans to achieve our objectives. Foremost among these is establishing contacts with our compatriots abroad and their organizations. For this we will sponsor visits of our industrialists and social activists to foreign countries. We have some experience in this regard. Tajik delegation of parliamentarians visited the autonomous regions of Seneszen and Uighur in the Peoples Republic of China, where they met and interacted with the members of their society including the Tajiks of the city of Urumchi and the suburbs of Tash Qurgan. They presented them copies of the works of Tajik writers and intellectuals, musical instruments and other gift items. It was agreed that these cultural exchanges should continue in future too.

We will also develop and expand contacts with businessmen and their organizations. We support plans that sensitize our expatriates to accord due respect to the Soviet Union and Tajikistan. Yet another task that we propose to undertake is to provide facilities to form organizations of culture and art, public and private libraries, elementary schools for learning mother tongue and assemblies of promising talented artists.

The Payvand will send copies of its publications on literature and current politics, dailies and journals pertaining to the history and society of Tajikistan to our counterparts. Cassettes of Tajik music and songs will also be sent to them. I must say in all fairness that we, too, have benefited from their contacts. We want to acquire copies of rare works of our ancestors that are in the hands of our expatriates. If an opportunity comes our way we would also like to float trade relations with our compatriots. We also intend inviting troupes of artists and musicians from our expatriate chapter to our republic. We also like to separately invite some people to whom we should assign the task of deliberating on vital social and political aspects of Tajikistan. One of our plans is to provide succor to the wards of our compatriots for receiving education in the institutions of higher learning of our republic. . The Payvand, in collaboration with a public enterprising association named Rodina, is about institute student scholarships.

Q: You have hinted at the publications of Payvand. What should we infer from that?

A: Payvand will bring out publications in Tajiki with Arabic script. if conditions permit, we shall also have publications in Arabic, and German languages, so that foreign readers can also have access and enjoy the literature. Apart from this, we plan to start a special program named *Seda-e Payvand* in the foreign service of Radio Tajikistan.

Q: Considering what you aspire to do in Payvand, your funds and man power are not adequate for implementing your plans Your plans cannot be carried out even by a department of the government.

A: Our entire team would comprise just eleven members. They are competent people and many of them know foreign languages. They are conversant with international practices. However, we do have expectations from the members of the association and social and creative organizations of our foreign compatriots.

Our organization's funding will come from its publications and other government's grant-in-aid to public organizations, voluntary membership of various public organizations of the Republic, gifts and endowments from expatriates and their organizations.

Q: Professor, Sir, we wish you and your team at Payvand success in accomplishing your noble and pious mission of forging understanding among human beings. On our part, we are glad to allocate one page of our journal *Tajikistan* for promoting the enviable objectives of Payvand.

A: Thanks. This is truly a generous offer. After all, connecting hearts and connecting generations is not the mission of Payvand alone. It is the duty of all well-wishing, humanistic, and peace-loving people.

(Interviewed by Karim Ya'qub)

_____

Tajik Association in America

Happily our readers are aware that in early autumn of the current year, an International Forum of Tajik-Farsi Speaking Peoples will meet in Dushanbe. The Organizing Committee of this important convention has begun its preliminary preparations.

The actual aim of the travel of Professor Muhammad Osimi, the President of Payvand organization, and the Affiliate of Farhangistan, together with the group of his colleagues to the United States of America, was to discuss the proposal of an international convention with friends there.

Recently, Muhammad Osimi spoke to a gathering of writers at Tajikistan Writers Union about his visit to the United States of America.

Academician Osimi said that more than two thousand Tajik emigrants were reported to be living in the city of New York. They migrated for various reasons. Most of them had been the members of 'Turkistan' organization. This powerful organization brought together some people of Trans-Oxiana. But owing to recent political developments in the Soviet Union, and the declaration of independence by the former republics of this Union, the viewpoint in regard to the Turkistan organization has changed considerably. Now these emigrants have decided to get into touch with their respective governments of the independent regions established on the basis of nationalities. This means that the Tajiks would get into touch with Tajikistan, Uzbeks with Uzbekistan and so forth and so on. I would like to draw to your attention to one particular point," said Osimi. Like us, the Tajiks here, the Tajik émigrés, also have a poor sense of self-identity.

In the first meeting between the representatives of Tajikistan and those of our compatriots in New York, Zahir Jan Ya'qubi, an American businessman, who hailed from Samarkand was elected President of American Tajik Association. The American Tajiks promised that in their next meeting they would choose their delegates to the World Association of Tajiks.

As M. Osimi mentioned, most of the Tajiks living in America have preserved their indigenous language and tradition. Not only that, some have preserved even the dialect of the particular region in Tajikistan from where they come. Our compatriots across the ocean are extremely happy with our country's independence. Some of them intend to help the country in its economic activities by making investments in Tajikistan. They would like to open factories jointly with the Tajiks. But some are still apprehensive of the aggressive control of the communists. Most of our compatriots abroad would like to have double citizenship, citizenship of the US as well as of Tajikistan. If the concerned authorities in Tajikistan accept this proposal then it will go in our interests. Or compatriots could travel to the land of their ancestors without much hassle, without going through complicated documentation processes and without having to waste precious time. This would lead to the creation of a bridge between the two countries. The number of Bukharan Jewish Tajiks, who have migrated to the US, is by no means small. They proudly call themselves Tajiks and are eagerly desirous of establishing contacts with the place of their birth. Most of them are energetic businessmen and their expertise could be of much benefit to our Republic. Musicians among the Bukharan Jews have formed a Union of Artists called *shashmaqam*. They occasionally perform for their community. We, too, were invited to one of their concerts. Its standard was very high.

It was during this journey that the Payvand delegation succeeded in establishing liaison between The Association of Tajiks and the US Association of Bukharan Jews. This was done with the intention of forging solid bilateral relationship between the two.

Continuing his interview at the Union of Writers, Osimi said that in the US, he was met and talked with the reputed Farsi poet Nadir Nadirpour, famous littérateur and the chief editor of the journal *Iranshinasi* Jalal Matini, eminent theatrical personality Mahmud Hakkak (the brother of well-known scholar of Farsi literature, Ahmad Karimi Hakkak), and eminent American scholars of Iranian origin such as Ehsan Yar Shatir, Ali Ja'afari and several others.

In these meetings, specific mention was made of the preparations for celebrating the millennium of *Shahnameh* of Ferdowsi, proposed for 1994 in Tajikistan. Mention was also made of the International Symposium on Farsi poetry to be held in 1993 and the commemorative function for Kamal Khujandi in 1995.

Reporter: Editor

Seda-e Mardum, February 21,1992, pp. 3-4

Payvand undertakes connecting for the unity of the nation

Interview with the icon of Tajik culture, Muhammad Osimi

Q: Respected Professor, people to people diplomacy is gaining ground all over the world. The Payvand organization headed by you is a direct beneficiary of this process. Your organization has been active for about two years in the past. Could you kindly list the tasks that have been accomplished during this period?

A: First of all we focused on collecting information about our community members scattered all over the four corners of the globe. We wanted to know the countries where they had taken shelter. Of course, we did have information about Tajik refugees in the neighboring countries, but we did not know the number of the Tajiks who had been sent on forced exile to different countries. We tried to acquaint them with our new republic in order to remove the sense of mistrust and fear from their minds. After my interaction with them, I could see that they have begun to believe that there is definitely a change in their Payvand considers its foremost and noble duty to work towards helping them in re-establishing contact with their kith and kin and their native land.

Har kasi ko dur mand az asli khwesh
Baz juyad rozgare waslih khwesh

One who is distanced from one's origin
Seeks the day of reunion with his origin

Through the instrumentality of Payvand, we have succeeded in making Dushanbe and Mazare Sharif brother cities. This friendly step of our organization received full support from Akramov, the Chairman of the Organizing Committee and other higher echelons of the administration. Today you find us happy and joyful on the expansion of our relations. The artist troupe Zeba performed twice in Mazare Sharif and Kabul and that was a source of happiness and enjoyment for our co-lingual fraternity. We are planning to send a delegation of folklore troupe *Ganjineh* to Afghanistan under the leadership of the famous artist Zafari Nozim. The monthly publication *Payvand* enjoys considerable influence and credibility with expatriate Tajiks. By no means is this a humble service that Payvand organization is rendering to the nation. This periodical publishing is a mutual publishing of the Union of Writers and our organization.

Q: It is a fact that Tajiks are dispersed in various countries from Japan to Indonesia and to the American continent. Payvand's mission is to connect them and to bring them together. Does the organization have any information about the number of Tajiks all over the world?

A: It is not easy to provide the exact number of ethnic Tajiks. Two thousand Tajiks are reported to be living in New York. There could be tens of thousands of them in Saudi Arabia. However, in other parts, their number is small. We have also been were informed of their presence UK, France and Turkey. We are trying to locate them. Once we are able to locate even one of them, we can reach others through that link.

Q: How does Payvand plan to meet with the Dari speaking peoples of Afghanistan who call themselves Tajiks and not Afghans? Their population is reported to be two or three times more than that of Tajiks of Central Asia. Apart from that we also know that Balkh, Herat, Ghazni and Kabul have been the ancient seats of Farsi language.

A: We shall have to differentiate between the Dari speaking people and the Tajiks of Afghanistan. The number of Dari or Farsi speaking peoples is very large. Perhaps more than 80 per cent population of that country speaks Farsi. The Hazaras also speak Farsi. A section of Pushto clans (perhaps in Kabul) also speaks Farsi. Again, by Farsi speaking alone cannot make a people into Tajiks. The Tajiks in that country are in themselves a nation with a long past. You are right in saying that their number is large. We are determined to strengthen our connections with the Tajiks. But that does not mean that we shall ignore the rest of Farsi speaking population. Those from among them, who come to us in Payvand and seek our support in furthering their trade or educational pursuits, comprise not only our co-linguist Tajiks but other nationalities as well.

Q: All the Central Asian Republics are now separate independent states. Payvand plans to establish cultural relations with co-linguists abroad. How is the organization envisaging relationship with local Central Asian Tajiks and how would it deal with Kazakhstan?

A: It is not hidden from anybody that from day one of the inception of Payvand, we have desired to have relations with the Tajiks in all the Central Asian Republics, including Kazakhstan. But for obvious reasons, top leadership adopted a lackadaisical attitude in this matter. Not only that, they even went to the length of calling it interference in the internal affairs of a neighboring state. Personally, I do not find any element of interference in the plans that we have announced. I am in favor of Uzbeks of Tajikistan establishing cultural relations with Uzbekistan, Turkmen with Turkmenistan and Kyrgyz with Kyrgyzstan. They should be able to benefit from the scientific and technical achievements of these republics. In the same way our republic should establish contacts with Tajik cultural centers in these Republics. Payvand has taken the initiative in this direction. We approached Tajik Centers in Uzbekistan by writing a letter to them. This was published in *Awaz-e Samarkand* and was read over the provincial television. We are planning a visit to those centers so that we can lend our helping hand for reviving and developing their language and culture. We plan to send teams of artists and littérateurs to these republics. In the month of November we were in Samarkand and we discussed that it would be feasible to organize an assembly of the Tajiks of Uzbekistan. Payvand is ready to take an active part in this mission.

Q: Have you been in touch with Farsi speaking people in Pakistan and Hindustan? Tajiks have been living in those regions for a long time. Many of them are reported to inhabit the northern parts of Pakistan. Once we heard a young girl of those areas speaking from Moscow television in her sweet and melodious Tajiki.

A: I have had personal contacts with the Farsi speaking people of Pakistan. I have inherited this noble tradition from late Babajan Ghafarov. I am friendly with a well-known scholarly person Hakim Muhammad Saeed, the Head of *Hamdard* Organization. Another close Pakistani friend of mine is the reputed archaeologist Ahmad Hasan Dani, who visited Dushanbe recently. Together with Muhammad Anwar Khan, the Vice Chancellor of Lahore University, he paid us a visit at Payvand. Anwar Khan is a Farsi speaking scholar and he informed us that Lahore University had a Department of Farsi language. In the round table conference to commemorate the 80th anniversary of Torsunzadeh, he spoke in chaste Farsi.

Many Farsi speaking people live in India as well. A conference of Persian teachers of Indian universities is organized annually in that country. They send us invitation letters to participate in those conferences. This year four persons from Tajikistan participated in that conference.

Q: You have recently returned from a visit to the United States of America. We understand you have done very creditable work for Payvand in that country.

A: The aim of our visit was to establish close contacts with the Tajik delegations there. Our contact with the Tajiks living in that country has a history. A World Fair was staged in Montreal, Canada in 1967. An official delegation of our republic had participated in it under the leadership of the then Prime Minister late Abdul Ahad Qahhar. The delegation also included leading artists like Mahmud Wahid, Malika-e Sabir, Jurabeg Murad, Ahmad Babaqol and Hanife-e Maulan. In one concert, I found some people listening to the recital with rapt attention and complete self-forgetfulness. Tears trickled down their cheeks. We came to know that they were our compatriots who had heard the melodies of Jurabeg

Murad and had traveled all the way from New York to Montreal to see him perform in person. They received us warmly and recorded Tajik melodies in cassettes. A few years later, when Jurabeg revisited New York, he met again with his old acquaintances. After returning home he told us that the number of Tajiks living in the US was much larger than what we had presumed. We dispatched an active delegation of Payvand to that country with the purpose of establishing contact with our brethren there. Our compatriots received us with warmth and affection and extended full hospitality to us. Among them were people from Samarkand, Bukhara, Khujand and Khatlan. We are particularly thankful to the rich business fraternity of the Jewish community originally from Samarkand. They are prepared to extend their support to the Tajik authorities for economic development of the Republic. Wherever we met with them, they spoke to us in sweet and delectable Tajiki language. Their youngsters have retained their customs, habits, faith and tradition. They like their native cuisine, *pilav* (national dish), *mantu* (lamb meat studded in baked dough), fried chicken, a variety of *kebob*, and *sambosa* studded with vegetables. They marry generally within their fold and rarely outside of it. That is also why we have stated that Payvand has also to look for brides and grooms. Previously an organization, *Turkistan,* was created for the union of Uzbeks and the Tajiks. In our meetings in the US, it was decided that a Tajik Association should be floated. Zahir Jan Ya'qubi, an energetic and outspoken ethnic Tajik was elected President of this Association. People, who had assembled for this purpose learnt about the formation of World Tajik Association and agreed to depute their representatives to the newly formed organization.

In New York, we had a number of meetings with Tajik speaking Jews. They comprise about 20 thousand members of the community and speak Farsi among themselves in their specific dialect. These have classical (Tajiki) singers among them. We happened to meet with our old acquaintances like Benyaminov, the former Professor at the College of Education and the famous stage actor Aronboev. In our meetings, we recounted the stories of co-existence between the Tajiks and the Jews. We talked about the contribution of Jewish community in the preservation of language and art of the Tajiks, particularly the *shashmaqam.* The Tajik Jewish people told us, "the culture of Tajiks is our culture and we are proud of it." We formed a branch of Payvand there, and Amnun Abayev, the well known businessman was elected its chairman. It was agreed that they would send their delegation to the convention of the Tajiks. The important thing was that our visit created possibilities of collaboration between the Tajik and Jewish traders.

Q: How are your relations with the Bukharan Jews living in Israel, Austria and other countries?

A: Honestly speaking, so far we have not been able to establish contact with them. We would like to send representatives of Payvand to Israel. However, let me say that we have close collaboration with the Association of Friends of Jewish Culture called *Hoverim,* which is headed by Professor Yohna Dadkhayev. This organization has requested us to provide them with office accommodation so that hand in hand we render service to people. We shall extend our hand of friendship to Hoverim.

Q: Have you tried to learn something from the experiment of similar conventions held in the Republics of Uzbekistan and Turkmenistan?

A: The World Uzbek Conference was held in Tashkent under the name of UL, and I participated in that. I had also addressed the audience. There were a good number of Tajik delegates from Afghanistan and

Saudi Arabia in that conference. We cultivated acquaintance with them and also sent a memorandum to our compatriots through them inviting them to participate in the World Tajik Convention. One of our officials went to Ashkabad in order to learn about the procedure adopted for creating the Turkmen Association. Their experience is certainly going to help us in the strengthening of our association.

Q: Who are at the top level of *Payvand*? Are there people from Samarkand and Bukhara? Is the politics of keeping them away still being pursued?

A: Payvand has six office bearers on its pay roll. But at the top level of the organization there are the erudite scholars of Tajikistan such as Laiq Sher Ali, Muhammad Jan Shukurov, Kamal Aini, Akbar Tursun, Damir Dostmuhammad, Ata Khan Latifi, Maysara Kalonova, Mazhabshah Mohabbatshah, Oktam Khaliq Nazar, Askar Hakim and Yohna Dadkhayev. It was not be possible to have members from Samarkand and Bukhara but this should be possible in future. We shall have members from those holy cities and we shall also set up ethnic Tajik centers there.

Q: Isn't it time when transit across the security posts along the Tajikistan — Afghanistan border were made easier and simpler and the iron wall standing between the two countries was demolished? How long shall we remain separated from our brethren?

A: We have made a proposal to the Parliament for double citizenship. Tajik people who are now citizens of Afghanistan could also become the citizens of Tajikistan. If that happens, they can travel without having to go through complicated formalities. Double citizenship has been accepted by many countries. Ukraine has also recently pasted this law.

Apart from this, the truth is that the time has come to make it possible to relax the existing transit rules, at least at some specific checkpoints. Business community should have freedom to travel. A climate of common economic interests needs to be created among Tajikistan, Iran, Afghanistan, Pakistan, Hindustan, and China. Now that we are basking in the sunshine of independence, no time should be wasted in fulfilling this task. At this point, I must add that our foreign ministry should view our organization's efforts in a positive manner.

Interviewed by Manuchehr Bazargan

———————————————————

Payam-e Dushanbe, June 27, 1992, p. 2

"We have great hopes from World Tajik Convention"

Muhammad Osimi

Interview

In the early September of this year (1992), a convention of World Tajik Association will be held in Dushanbe. This venture is of extraordinary historical importance for the social and economic life of our Republic. The sponsor of this peoples' world forum is the organization of cultural relations with foreign countries called Payvand, which is headed by outstanding erudite scholar and academician of the Academy of Sciences Tajikistan, Professor Muhammad Osimi. In an interview with our reporter, Professor Osimi answered many of his questions. We reproduce below a part of this conversation.

Q: Professor, Sir, May I request you to tell our readers something about the purpose and objectives of Payvand. What have been its achievements during one year of its existence?

A: A group of intellectuals from within the country had expressed the feasibility of establishing the organization. Such organizations existed previously in all the Republics of the erstwhile Soviet Union. Unfortunately, in our Republic our former leadership had a different view on this. They considered the inception of the World Association of Tajiks as something nationalistic. We made this venture with the purpose of establishing multi-sided relations with our compatriots. We have an objective and that is to revive the broken relations between the Tajik peoples.

The once expansive land of our forefathers, the vast Tajik Empire has fallen. We have now to be contented with only a small territory. Today, our nation stands separated owing to the re-drawing of political boundaries of various states. I cast a glance over Afghanistan, Iran, Uzbekistan, China, Kyrgyzstan, Turkmenistan and Kazakhstan where a large number of Tajiks live. Apart from this, during the seventy years of Soviet rule, a large number of our compatriots left their native land for a variety of reasons. Most of them lost their lives in despair of their native land, for being far away far away from their homes and their kith and kin. Their children remember their ancestors and nurse in their hearts the love of their land. Therefore, we think it a noble task to attract their attention to Tajikistan.

During the year we have been on, which is not too long a period, we invited the delegations of foreign-based Tajiks to Dushanbe. We also travelled to foreign lands. Some of our guests were apprehensive lest their name and those of their kith and kin were made public. But the changes that have occurred in our Republic have instilled confidence in them. They have come to believe that Tajikistan is truly a sovereign state.

We have made specific efforts to ascertain the number of Tajiks living in various countries of the world and introduce Payvand organization to them. We wanted our compatriots to know that an organization in Tajikistan is ready to help them to get connected with their kith and kin in Tajikistan.

I would like to mention here that Tajiks, no matter in whatever country they live in, do pay special attention to Tajikistan. They consider it the home of their hopes. They are glad that Tajikistan has begun to take steps of a long march towards real independence. However, they have anxieties too. One anxiety is that after wriggling out of the domination of one super power, they may fall into the clutches of another super power. They made no bones about it while talking to us about these apprehensions and they were serious about this.

For many years, relations between our Republic and Afghanistan were not smooth. Because of persuasion "brother – cities" status was established between Dushanbe and Mazar-e Sharif. You may be surprised to know that we had brother-city relations with cities in Europe and the US, but not with cities in our neighboring country, with which we have commonality of language and culture. For example, with Afghanistan and Iran, we did not have correct cultural, spiritual and economic relationship. We have, therefore, proposed an agreement for establishing brother-city relationship with some Iranian cities.

Payvand also sponsored the visits abroad of the troupe of artists. This will receive our serious attention, in days to come. Art is one of the powerful instruments for promoting mutual understanding. It helps people come together. Apart from this, we can also create a link between our businessmen and medium sized traders, by introducing them to each other. Tajik business magnates and traders living in foreign countries can support the economic development of our republic. There is a good number of Tajiks in almost all countries. Nearly two thousand of them live in New York City alone. Apart from this, more than twenty thousand Tajik speaking Jews living in that country have rendered valuable service in protecting our culture, especially *shashmaqam*.

Q: Time is running fast. September is not far away. May I request you to apprise us about your preparedness for the World Tajik Forum.

A: We had a number of ideas. Some of our colleagues suggested organizing the Forum simultaneously with the Navroz festival. The Council of Ministers, too, was reported to have agreed to this proposal. However, we took stock of the situation in its totality, and then decided to hold the session in the first half of the month of September. I think this time of the year will suit the distinguished guests. The Council of Ministers, too, has approved it.

We have selected a group of 240 Tajik compatriots residing in various countries of the world. Letters of invitation have been sent to most of them. However, invitations have not been sent to guests from Afghanistan as yet because of the political situation there. Our Afghan friends will receive the invitation letters in near future. We are also sending invitation letters to our Iranian brethren.

Sometimes, we hear discordant notes in the form of objections. For example, why should not the venture be called Forum for World Co-linguists in stead of World Tajik Forum? I would like to make it clear that we extend invitations only on behalf of the government of our republic, but our co-linguists have not been left out. During the course of the convention, we plan to float a scientific symposium also. The topic approved for the symposium is "The Contribution of Iranian race to human civilization". This gives us space to invite scholars from various countries of the world, especially from Iran, for participation in its deliberations. Delegations of Tajiks from Uzbekistan, Kyrgyzstan, Kazakhstan, Turkmenistan, Russia, Ukraine and Baltic Republics will be invited to participate. We have also invited scholars who are involved in the study of history and culture of our ancestors. I have scholars like Erji Bechka and Manfred Lawrence in my minds who have worked for introducing our national culture to the Westerners. Distinguished Pakistani scholar Hakim Muhammad Saeed has accepted our invitation, and we are about to send invitations to Burhanu'd-Din Rabbani and Ahmad Shah Masud of Afghanistan. Outstanding political personalities of Iran will also be invited to grace our convention with their presence.

The Forum will have two sections, one will be of the businessmen and traders who will interact with the Collective Farm leaders of the Republic, and the second will be the section of scholars and cultural icons. It would be a fit occasion to install the statue of Firdowsi in the Freedom Square during the convention so that have addressed the matter of providing comfortable accommodation to our guests and respond to their desire of sight seeing. We shall arrange their visit to the provinces and regions, to the cities of Samarkand and Bukhara. May be the guests have their kith and kin in the suburban areas. They might like to meet with them, to know about their welfare and pay a visit to the resting place of their ancestors.

We intend to initiate the formation of an international organization of Farsi speaking peoples for studying our common cultural fund. We could possibly have a committee for common terminology. It has been my cherished desire to have such a committee. Fifteen years ago, when I was on a tour of Iran, this subject was brought up for discussion. Professor Khanlari and other scholars of Iran had supported this proposal. It is a matter of great satisfaction that with the initiative taken by Iranian scholars recently, a special meeting was held regarding the terminology. The eminent scholar Muhammad Jan Shukurov and his delegation participated from our Republic.

The Joint Committee of Farsi Teachers has been holding its annual meetings in Delhi for a long time. If such a committee is formed in Dushanbe, it would be in the interests of our people.

The difficulties that we face in regard to the development of language are also the share of scholars in Afghanistan and Iran. Literary language has to be easy, smooth and sweet. All Farsi speaking people ought to make efforts to resolve whatever difficulties are in the way. We should learn good things from each other without giving ourselves up to imitation. It is our pious duty to protect the internationally standardized language. Had we not been the inheritors of a great literature, we might have today needed to speak to our blood brethren through an interpreter.

For the sake of unity the memorandum submitted by the organization to the people of Tajikistan has been accepted to by all Tajiks in the world. We have great expectations from Payvand organization. Some people say that we are not concerned about the Tajiks and that we go about roaming in the world. But I find a really good connection between the two aspects of this question. I think the more we extend relations with the Tajiks abroad the more it will benefit our country.

Market economy and rise in the prices of consumer goods have adversely affected the productive activity of the organization. Up to this day our staff traveled abroad without encountering financial difficulties. I visited the US with funds provided by our compatriots there. UNESCO funded my visits to Hindustan and Pakistan because I happened to be the President of the Organization for the Study of Central Asian Civilization. While addressing issues before the UNESCO, I gave due importance to the *Payvand* organization too. But from now onwards it will be difficult for us to send delegations to foreign countries.

In view of severe financial constrains, it is important that citizens, factories, foundations, and collective farms come forward with financial assistance to the organization. Some industrialists had promised to contribute money to the Forum. Some even advertised in newspapers that they had made financial contributions but not a single penny has been received by us till now.

The type of linguistic and cultural conclaves that we propose to hold in Tajikistan, have already been elaborately organized at a high level in the Republics of Turkmenistan, Tataristan, Uzbekistan, and other places. Organizing a world conference is not an easy task. Keeping in view the Tajik tradition of not to send our guests empty handed, we have decided to arrange some humble gifts for our guests. Some of these are almost ready For example, we had placed an order with the Tursunzadeh Chinaware Factory for manufacturing chinaware items bearing the legend of the *Payvand* organization. The stuff is ready for delivery. Yet another humble gift that we intend to give to our guests is a volume titled An *Anthology of Tajik Poems*. It contains selections from the poetic compositions of contemporary Tajik poets. A volume titled *Tajikan* authored by the well-known archaeologist Ya'qub Zadeh will be on the stands by the time the conference commences. A documentary film will also be made. All these activities need money.

Q: We understand that extending relations with emigrant Tajiks will be of immense benefit to our republic.

A: Of course it will be and has many aspects. However, the spiritual relationship is our priority. When we propose these possibilities, we feel that the Tajiks are not alone. It is a boon not to feel left out and isolated.

Payvand attaches great importance to the awakening of the sentiments of national consciousness and self-realization. For thousands of years we were subjugated by foreigners, which severely shattered our national consciousness. Things came to such a pass that the Tajiks hesitated to call themselves Tajiks. This phase has passed by. Now is the time for reconstruction. Financial support to our nation will certainly enhance the economy of our country. It is important to collaborate with those who have the capital to invest and those who are engaged in trade and commerce.

We yearn for our brethren to whom we are bound by common culture and language. The same is true of them too. When we displayed our monthly magazine *Payvand* to our compatriots in the US, they rubbed it to their eyes, demonstrating nostalgia for their ancestral land. We propose to bring it out every month.

History tells us that expansion of knowledge and culture has materialized during the times when there was cooperation among the people. If the Samanid rule had not held sway over Greater Khurasan, and had it not established links with all Eastern powers, we would neither have had Rudaki nor Abu Ali Ibn Sina. Therefore, I insist that the more we come close to our co-lingual fraternity the more chances we will get to move forward. In particular, it is essential for us to establish relations with Iran, Afghanistan, Pakistan and Hindustan that are dimensional.

Q: We are of the opinion that Tajikistan should not remain unconcerned about the fate of Tajiks living outside our national boundaries. According to received reports, the condition of Tajiks living in Uzbekistan is not that good. How can Payvand reach and support them? There is the Autonomous Region of Karakalpakistan in the Republic of Uzbekistan whose people speak Turkish. In Samarkand and Bukhara, Tajiks are in a majority. Would it not be feasible that for the sake of preservation of their language and national culture, these regions are converted into autonomous regions or republics?

A: We have close relations with Tajik cultural centers in Uzbekistan and are not neutral in regard to the future of the Tajiks there. We have sent letters to the leadership of this republic on behalf of Payvand organization and we have already heard from the Minister of Education of Uzbekistan, with regard to the condition of secondary and higher secondary schools of Tajiks and the department of Tajiki in their universities. As far as the autonomy of those regions is concerned, we should not try to interfere in the internal affairs of a sovereign state.

Q: The political and economic condition of our republic is critical, and there is an apprehension of the dismemberment of Tajikistan. What do we need to maintain national unity and territorial integrity of the republic?

A: Yes, there is an apprehension, but we ought not to exaggerate it. I have shared food with the Tajiks of Qaratigin, Badakhshan, Khatlan, Vakhsh, Zarafshan and Khujand, not once or twice but throughout my life. I know the character and the behavior of these people very well. Most of them are desirous of the solidarity of the republic. On that basis I can guarantee that the sagacious people of these regions will not allow our small and dear country to get parceled into pieces. Partition means losing the government and the destruction of our nation.

Now the question is: What should we do to preserve the solidarity and integrity of our republic? Before anything else, we must learn to speak the language of wisdom and not of gun. Where obstinacy and emotions rule the roost, the path leads only to hell. In a democratic society there is a plurality of ideas and truth surfaces only after a sensible debate. Of course, the target should be one and that is solidarity and unity. We have been a witness to the authority of one party arrangement, which cannot help a society move towards development. Our government needs to have a clearly defined target, an action plan and strength to implement it. It is said that the government stands in the need of the politics of wisdom. Today, in Dushanbe we have formed unions of compatriots. We would appreciate their leaders sitting round a table to deliberate on the question of national unity and find solutions.

At the moment, conditions in some places are not satisfactory. Innocent people are getting killed. It is the urgent responsibility of the President and the Government of Tajikistan to see that armed groups in the country are disarmed forthwith. We would appreciate if the government imposed a ban on them till the time of holding the convention (this happens in extraordinary conditions like war and some crisis). If conditions of turmoil continue, our guests may have second thoughts about visiting Dushanbe. Today some of our compatriots make telephonic enquiries about the holding of the convention. Some elements indulge in exaggerating the situation. This dissuades our guest from coming within the country the old system of governance is no more in place. Those who wishfully hope the return of that era are making a big mistake. Only a big program of economic and social reforms can pull us out of the morass of economic and political crisis.

With regard to the governing structure of our republic I can say that we should not imitate this or that pattern of governance, but look for the best in all patterns and then look for a path that suits our interests best. Whenever this question was posed to me in Pakistan I quoted the following verses of Iqbal:

Tarash az tesheh-e khud jadeh-e khwesh
Be rah-e digaran raftan azaab ast
Gar az dast-e tu kar-e nadir ayad
Gunahi ham agar bashad sawab ast

Make your path with your own pickaxe
It is a pain to go along the path made by others
Should you do something rare in your life?
It will be a virtue even if it is a patent sin

All that needs to be added is that in any society, and more especially in a society focusing on the rights of people, it is important that the law is given due respect. Everybody should consider himself equal before law.

Q: Professor, Sir, you have recently returned from your travels to Hindustan and Pakistan. Would you kindly give us some of your impressions?

A: In Hindustan and Pakistan much attention is paid to our independent republic. Professor Nurul Hasan, the outstanding scholar and political figure of India, is an old friend of late Bobojon Ghafurov. After the conclusion of a weeklong meeting of UNESCO, Nurul Hasan invited me to travel to the State of West Bengal and be his guest for a week or more. I agreed to accept his invitation even though I was supposed to take a flight to Portugal for participation in a scientific conference, for which the hosts had already sent me the air ticket

There he introduced me to industrialists, traders, and intellectuals, especially the Iranologists with whom I had warm and useful exchange of views. Investors and business magnates asked me about the needs of Tajikistan, and expressed their willingness to extend their support. One businessman wanted to know if he could export the products of his factory to Tajikistan.

These meetings clarified that Hindustan enjoyed age-old relations with the land of the Tajiks. For eight centuries, Farsi language, especially of the *velayat-e bala* meaning Trans-Oxiana (*ma'wara' an-nahr*) had remained the language of the court and of science and culture in Hindustan. Thousands of rare manuscripts were written in this language and are preserved in the famous Oriental Library of Calcutta and elsewhere. Among these treasures, I had the opportunity to see an illustrated manuscript copy of *Shahnameh* of Ferdowsi, the *Khamsa* of Nizami, *Khavar Nameh* and an authentic manuscript copy of the *Tadhkiratu'l-Shu'ara* of Daulatshah Samarkandi.

Nurul Hasan said that he had staked all his credibility to the expansion of relations between India and Tajikistan and to provide selfless support to Tajik friends. In a formal reception hosted in my honour, he pointed towards me and told the audience that Tajikistan was in his heart.

During my stay in Hindustan, local newspapers flashed the news of a possible visit of the President of Tajikistan to New Delhi, which unfortunately did not take place.

During my informal meetings with the Indian friends, we also talked about the life style, habits and manners of our peoples. In one of these meetings, my Indian friends told me a surprising story about the people living in a gorge somewhere to the north of the country where apricots formed the main diet of the local population.

The people of the region were handsome and physically very strong and never suffered a heart attack. They have a long life span. Therefore apricots are very beneficial for promotion of good health and a longer span of life. As I heard this story, I felt somewhat sad that we had forgotten the tradition of our ancestors and had almost given up the growing of apricots.

After completing my travel in India, I went to Pakistan on the invitation of my friend Ahmad Hasan Dani. I stayed there for ten days. I addressed a gathering at the Iqbal Academy in Lahore. I had an exchange of ideas with the lovers of Iqbal's verses and my speech was on the impact of Iqbal's poetry on the spiritual life of Tajiks. If I said that Lahore was one of the centers of Tajik civilization, I hope I did not make a wrong statement. It should be mentioned that for the first time the Tajik poet Mir Saeed Mir Shakar introduced Iqbal to the Tajik readership. Some among the audience put several questions to me about how the people in Tajikistan rated the great thinker. I provided them full information about the centenary celebration of this great intellectual in Dushanbe, emphasizing Iqbal's contribution towards the awakening and self-realization among the Tajiks.

My meetings and interaction with the scholars and intellectuals of Pakistan were the sweetest and choice moments of my stay. The intellectuals in Lahore skipped their important engagements and talked to me on very interesting things.

In Islamabad, I had a long meeting with the President of the Republic, Ghulam Ishaque Khan. He referred to a thousand year old relations between us and said that Pakistan was ready to extend all help to Tajikistan. This meeting was telecast in Pakistan and after that a large number of people came to see me. They wanted to be invited to the Tajik forum. I was proud to realize that our small Republic enjoys such respect in that country. After all, the total population of our Republic is almost equal to the population of the city of Lahore.

At the same time, when disturbing news arrived from Dushanbe, it made me very sad. My Pakistani friends sympathized with me and tried to assuage my feelings by telling me that that was a temporary thing and would soon be over. They had full confidence in the wisdom and sagacity of our people. I consider it my duty to extend condolence to the families of the martyred people and those who have been the victims of natural calamity. I extend to them the sympathy of my friends, colleagues and my own.

In the assemblies and meetings in universities and in the gatherings of intellectuals in India and Pakistan, I spoke both in English and Farsi. I tried to present in detail the contribution of the Tajiks to the history of human civilization.

Q: Some of our friends, after returning from their travels in these neighboring countries said that the standard of living there was higher than in ours. Is this true?

A: The standard of living in Pakistan is slightly higher than that in Hindustan. In both countries, markets, stores and shops are packed with commodities, edibles and other goods. But abundance of consumer goods does not necessarily indicate a higher standard of living of all people. During my stay in India, I travelled by train from Delhi to Calcutta to see from closer quarters the life of rural and urban people. Frankly speaking, the condition of people in rural areas of this vast country is not that good. Our villages have made good progress. I have also travelled by train from Tashkent to Dushanbe. We live in paradise. We have all possibilities that are necessary for raising the living standard of the people of our republic.

I would like to add that in Hindustan and Pakistan, there is freedom of public expression. One does not come across political or ethnic prejudice. But of course some incidents of ethnic and religious conflicts have taken place, especially in Kashmir, Sindh and Punjab. Pakistan is an Islamic state but the followers of other faiths are free in that country. In Pakistan, apart from Muslims, there are Christians, Jews, Buddhists and people of others faiths. Their places of worship stand in close proximity to each other. Dress code is free and people mind only their business. I found women in Islamabad and Karachi clad in western attire. Nobody castigates them.

Q: Professor, you have visited a number of world capitals. How would you like to see the capital of our republic?

A: Whenever friends pay us a visit, they are eloquent about the beauty of Dushanbe. Evidently, they do not know our shortcomings. Of all the capital cities that I have visited, I like Islamabad the best. It is a comparatively recently built capital, and as such, a modern city. Its streets are straight and lined with greenery, thus increasing its beauty. What attracts the onlooker is abundance of goods and absence of want among the people. Stores are packed with goods of all sorts. May be market economy will bring affluence to our cities also.

Reservation in hotels is easy and the service available in them is of the highest order. In Delhi, a new hotel by the name Taj Palace has come up. It is rated one of the best hotels in the world. It has a number of spacious and airy saloons and the UNESCO meeting was held in one. These saloons with attractive names like Mumtaz Mahal, Roshan Ara, Jahan Ara etc. are floored in exquisite marble. Amidst its gardens around the complex, there are beautiful pathways, and one hears in its spacious lifts classical western music. This is found in the hotels in Pakistan too. Attendants in the hotels are all smiles and courtesy.

The condition of our hotels is very bad and we have a lot of work to do on this. In Islamabad, plantation of trees has been made with much artistry and fountains abound in the city. Incidentally, love for fountains and laying the gardens have been inherited by the locals from the descendants of the house of Timur in India. Shalimar Garden in Lahore is wonderful. It was the beloved capital of the house of Timurids in India:

Lahore ra ba jan barabar kharideh-em
Jan dadeh-em o jannat-e digar kharideh em

(We have bought Lahore with a price equal to life
We have given life but bought a second paradise)

Shalimar Garden comprises three parts. Part one named Farah Bakhsh has shady trees and flowers of different hues. The second part has space large enough for sitting and resting and the third part called Faiz Baksh carries a variety of fruit trees grapevines, peaches, almonds, plums, cherries, mulberries, apricots, etc. There are 452 fountains in this spacious garden, which have been running for 300 years. It has ponds and streams of water. Lamps illuminate the fountains during night and this present very attractive view. Emperor Jahangir laid the Shalimar Garden in the vicinity of Srinagar and it excels the Shalimar garden of Lahore. That garden has seven terraces. There are beautiful gardens in Delhi too. If due importance was given to the laying of gardens in our capital city, its beauty would be enhanced considerably.

Another thing that I would like to mention is the truthfulness of the people. Citizenry in these countries does tell lies or break promises. Once they have made a promise, they will fulfill it. My friends had promised to send me some books and they did. They even sent a letter to confirm that I have received those books.

Q: Professor, Sir, we understand that you are fond of the daily *Payame Dushanbe*. What would you have to say about our paper?

A: I read *Payam-e Dushanbe* with gusto. I had myself proposed the publication of the book *Payambar*. We should continue publishing works of this type. Your daily newspaper does justice to daily events. This is extraordinarily important, and this trend should continue. In my opinion criticism should be selfless and justice should be done to the events. We should not limit ourselves to the present; the future too needs to be taken care of. Young journalists should not forget that they will be under the scrutinizing eye of future generations, and their activities and contributions will be subjected to evaluation. Therefore, it is pertinent that they keep in mind how best they can serve the present and the future of the nation. My only wish is that the *Payam* takes due care of spiritual enrichment of the people of our republic.

Thank you for very warm and meaningful exchange of views. We wish you success in your noble effort of contributing to the progress of our society.

Aziz Salal
Correspondent *Payam-e Dushanbe*

Jamhooriyat, August 28, 1992

"Let coming of guests to Tajikistan be an auspicious event"

Muhammad Osimi

Our countrymen are aware that in coming days the first ever convention of World Tajiks and Compatriots Abroad will be held in Dushanbe, the capital of Tajikistan. This imposing function set afoot by untiring efforts of our country's noble sons and daughters is expected to prepare ground for the people of contemporary world to see the Tajik people and its country from very close quarters. A little while ago, I was one among the reporters present at the meeting of the organizing committee. I am convinced that the organizers have made stupendous effort for making the impressive function a great success. Professor Muhammad Osimi, the President of Payvand organization heads the team for Cultural Relations of Tajikistan with Compatriots Abroad.

We are about to complete one year of our independence. We established contact with Professor Osimi in connection with the first convention of World Tajiks and Compatriots Abroad and requested him to express himself on the subject for the benefit of our readers. Here is summary of the interview he gave us.

Q: Let me begin by conveying thanks from the contributors and sympathizers of the Daily *Jamhooriyat* for initiating the noble cause. We are hopeful that the organization will make positive contribution towards the progress of Tajikistan.

A: Thank you. We are confident that it will.

Q: Only a few days are left for the convention to begin. Please describe the preparations underway.

A: Yes, we are fast approaching the day of the commencement of this big function. The organizers are in the grip of excitement. Personally, I believe that the organization will contribute to the forging of unity among the parties and the movement of the people. With the help and cooperation of their members, it will be possible to restore normalcy. If this possibility becomes a reality, then we can presume that the function will have reached its real splendor. The primary duty of each of us is that before anything else the situation in Tajikistan is brought back to normal.

Till now, we have distributed about 400 invitation letters. It is gratifying that we continue to receive encouraging responses. These messages indicate that a number of delegations, legislators and independent visitors in different foreign countries have already proceeded to the ancient land of Tajikistan. I would like to reiterate that we have made necessary preparations to receive the guests and finalized the agenda of the convention. We are confident that hospitable and enlightened people of Tajikistan will lend us their support in this noble mission and create conducive conditions for decent and befitting conclusion of this national function.

Q: Were the Farsi speaking people of the world and our compatriots abroad aware of our program of holding this grand convention?

A: In the summer this year, *Payvand*, the Cultural Relations Organization of Tajikistan with Compatriots Abroad, had many visitors. Representatives of organizations and groups of Tajiks in foreign countries from all parts of the world visited us. We met with the leader of the American Tajik Association chief Mir Muhammad Zahir Ya'qubi. We also had meetings with the representatives of Tajik and Uzbek migrants in Saudi Arabia. *Hoverim* an organization of the Jews, extended help to us for inviting the Jewish compatriots now based in Israel and the US. From Pakistan, we have not only invited the Tajiks stationed there but also some prominent persons of the country. They are eager to acquaint themselves with the history of ancient Tajikistan, and to see that all its problems are resolved. It is satisfying to note that in these meetings we were able to deliberate on how similar conventions can be organized in future.

Q: Professor, Sir, we would appreciate if you tell us about the program of the convention for the information of our readers.

A: The first thing we would like to bring to the knowledge of the participants in the first convention of World Tajiks and Compatriots Abroad is the purpose of Tajik International and the founding of Centre for Teaching Farsi Language. We have drawn necessary documentation for the purpose.

According to the program, the *Payvand* will, with the initiative of the Academy of Sciences, organize a scientific international symposium in Dushanbe. The guests will also visit the towns and regions of Tajikistan and acquaint themselves with historical places and the life of the people. They will visit scientific foundations; catch up with writers, poets, artists, social workers and business magnates and small traders. A learned Tajik scholar, Muhammad, has produced a scholarly work titled *Tajikistan*. Very soon this interesting publication will be in our hands. The statue of Abul Qasim Firdowsi in the Freedom Square will be unveiled with proper ceremony and this will be a gift for the people on this occasion.

The inaugural ceremony of the grand function will take place in the Barbod Hall in Dushanbe. The most accomplished artists of Tajikistan will entertain the guests with vocal and instrumental music.

Q: Thanks for lovely conversation, dear Professor. What are your expectations from this convention?

A: We hope the footsteps of our guests prove auspicious for us and this organization contributes to the prosperity of the people of our country.

Interviewed by Muhammad Egamzad,
News Reporter, *Jamhooriyat*.

"Unfortunate is the nation that remains isolated" Osimi

Q: Respected Professor, the time for inauguration of the convention of Tajiks and Compatriots Abroad is close at hand. Can we say with confidence that Tajikistan is fully prepared to host this conference?

A: Tajikistan and her people are always prepared for such celebrations. Among the virtues of Tajiks is to seek and care for their brethren whom destiny separated from us and to know about their welfare and whereabouts. The International Convention has actually been proposed on the request of the general public. Therefore, our government, leaders, party activists and political organizations are conscious of their responsibilities. This is the first conclave of our compatriots who had to leave their home owing either to the vagaries of time or the excesses of governing apparatus. Many of them carried the dream of returning to their native land to their graves. Their progeny have inherited from them their love for the native land yearning to kiss the soil of their ancestors, and are desirous of meeting with their near and dear ones. We cannot disappoint them. As we see, there is no satisfactory stability in the country. Therefore, it is important that all politicians and their followers, irrespective of their political interests, come together to accord warm welcome to our guests. They should live up to the noble traditions of our illustrious ancestors, be warm and sincere to our guests.

We can know each other far better through the instrumentality of this convention. The World Forum of Tajiks once again provides us — the internal Tajiks — an opportunity to think of the company we should keep. We are at present a small nation but with a long history. However, the events of recent years show that our ancient history and rich culture have become a weight on our shoulders. May God be just to us all, small and big, politician and the soil turning peasant, communist and democrat and not let this weight of our history fall off our shoulders.

Let me now say something about preparedness for the convention. I must say it firmly that we are prepared for it. The first letters of invitation were sent to the kith and kin of those who had expressed their desire to participate in the assembly. Four hundred of them have already been invited. We expect that at least half of them will show up. In particular we are expecting guests from Iran and Afghanistan. We have some apprehension about those who are from distant countries. Some of them in the US, Europe and Saudi Arabia rang me up and imploringly asked me about the situation in Tajikistan and the welfare of its people. We have realized one more thing in recent days: Fears about internal insecurity have been deliberately exaggerated. People who write letters or make telephonic calls have only one question: Who can guarantee security in Tajikistan?

In connection with the holding of the Forum, several resolutions and legal documents have been worked out. One of the resolutions asks for legal documentation according to which the World Centre of Tajiks would be incepted. In order to meet this requirement, we prepared the draft of the code of conduct for Tajik International, which has to receive the approval of the Forum. One draft of appeal to the people of Tajikistan and another to the Tajiks world over has been prepared. In this connection, a volume about the ethno genesis of Tajiks and compiled by the well-known historian and archaeologist Yusuf Shah

Ya'qub Shah is under preparation in Iran. Copies of the book will be sold in Iran and Tajikistan. Copies of this work will also be gifted to the guests as souvenirs. We have also agreed to hold an international symposium "Iran's contribution to human civilization" during the convention on the theme.

Q: Indeed, this symposium is something like an assembly within an assembly. Can you tell us more about this?

A: With pleasure. You are very right: this symposium is an assembly within an assembly. Actually we wanted the Forum to be an assembly of Tajik and Farsi speaking peoples of the world, but our Iranian and Afghani brethren suggested that the matter be discussed at a higher level among the governments of Tajikistan, Iran and Afghanistan to take upon them the responsibility of organizing the conference jointly. Therefore, if the conference was to be organized solely by Tajikistan then, evidently, this had to be the World Tajik Conference and Tajikistan would be inviting compatriots abroad as guests to the function. After some discussion on various aspects of the matter, the latter option was considered feasible. Therefore, to make sure that our Iranian brethren do not remain outside the ambit of the conference, it was decided that a symposium on the topic of "Contribution of Iranians to Human Civilization" should also figure in the conference. But, of course, it has to be understood in its wider meaning to include the contribution of the Tajiks as well. A large number of eminent and reputed scholars from Iran, Afghanistan, Europe, the US as well as the Iranologists from the republics of erstwhile Soviet Union have expressed their desire to participate in the symposium. More than one hundred scholars and researchers have sent in their scholarly papers and monographs to the Organizing Committee of the organization. I should like to mention here that the conference is being organized under the auspices of Payvand with the collaboration of Tajikistan Academy of Sciences and the Friendship Society. The chairmanship of the Organizing Committee rests with the Deputy Prime Minister of the Republic, respectable Habibullah Saeedmuradov. The task of conducting the function is to be undertaken by the Academy of Sciences of Tajikistan. Its representative, the intrepid scholar and music director Askar Ali Rajabov, is taking great pains and attending to the minutest detail of the symposium. He has proceeded to Iran for printing the scholarly papers, theses and monographs in Farsi, English, and Russian languages.

Q: Does the program of the conference envisage only holding of the formal assemblies and scholarly meetings?

A: Why should it be confined to that? It has been planned that the guests will get the opportunity of visiting the cities and villages of various parts of Tajikistan such as Khatlan, Vakhshanzamin, Khujand, Badakhshan, Rasht, Zarafshan, Darwaz and Hisar. Those who have located their kith and kin in one or the other nook of Tajikistan may like to visit those families. They would like to meet in an atmosphere of freedom. However, taking into account the current situation in the republic, this may not be easy. We hope the situation returns to normal and a large number of our compatriots return home without getting disappointed. We are also desirous that relations between Tajikistan and our neighboring Republic of Uzbekistan become as cordial as were in earlier days so that our guests are able to visit Samarkand and Bukhara, the ancient fabulous cities of their ancestors.

Q: Should we understand that a change in the program of the conference is connected with a change in the political situation of the republic?

A: Yes. We have, no doubt, chalked the program of the International Forum but its full implementation depends on the political situation of Tajikistan and a change in the relationship between Tajikistan and Uzbekistan. Honestly speaking, the existing prospect of relationship between the two has been the cause of much concern to us. Their ongoing relation is not only disturbing for the leadership of our republic but also exerting a profound impact on the destiny of the Tajik people. Tajiks who speak derogatory words about Uzbekistan forget that relations between the two peoples are rooted in history. As blood brothers for centuries they have been part and parcel of each other. Is it possible to tear them apart? Tearing away the nail from the fingertip will result in the flow of blood. We should not forget that there are a few million Tajiks in Uzbekistan. If we strain our mutual relations, what will happen to them? If we are true patriots and nationalists, then we should care for all the Tajiks and not of one district or one area alone. If we call ourselves a nation with several thousand years' old history and civilization, then we should care for the Tajiks wherever they are living, in Uzbekistan, Kazakhstan, Kyrgyzstan or Turkmenistan and also the ones living in foreign countries. They are all our brethren! We claim to be the inheritors of the rich culture of Samarkand and Bukhara but sometimes we annoy the people of those cities. Why should it happen? Indiscreet words and deeds of some of our brethren surprise me a great deal. If we attribute the people, against whom we raise a finger, to this or that place and region and area, and thus annoy them, who will go with us? A thousand years ago Abu Rayhan Biruni said that prejudice makes the seeing eye blind and the hearing ears deaf. I am amazed that some of us, who pretend to care for the nation and claim to be its patrons, are blind and deaf towards the issue.

Q: Holding of a conference entails a good deal of expenditure. Have you been able to raise enough funds to meet all the expenses?

A: I am sorry to say that at the moment we don't have adequate funds. We have almost exhausted our savings. But I am hopeful that our business community, traders, foundations, and collective farms will demonstrate their frugality and will come forward to make their contribution to this noble task. In this context, I had a meeting with Habibullah Saeed Muradov along with some business magnates. Some of them have already made contribution to the organization according to their means. For example, the Construction and Industrial Bank has contributed one hundred thousand rubles (Russian currency). The Senez Cooperative Production has contributed 150 thousand rubles, Karakul Development Union of the Republic has contributed 120 thousand rubles "Intergraph" company, and Electric Equipment Factory has contributed 50 thousand rubles.

We hope that other industrialists and factory owners will follow suit. Likewise, despite severe economic and financial constraints, we expect a solid contribution from the Government of the Republic.

A major part of our funds will be spent on travel expenses of the guests. We have told them to arrange for their return tickets on their own. We believe that they fully understand our monetary constraints. Obviously, they would not mind spending from their pocket for the love of visiting their native land and their kith and kin. On an average we shall be spending around a thousand rubles per head per day, which is quite expected for a conference of this type. But paucity of funds induces us to seek contributions.

The guests of the conference are the guests of Tajikistan. When a guest from a long distance comes to the house of a Tajik, he kills a sheep following the age-old tradition of hospitality. Why should we not kill that sheep and cow and invite everybody to partake of feast?

Q: Professor, sir, in your capacity as the head of *Payvand*, what are your expectations from the World Tajik Forum?

A: Let me say that we not only aspire to gain cultural advantages from this Forum but also seek economic dividends. Among the invites are business magnates, traders and reputed experts. Our business community can derive positive benefits from this opportunity. Our people will establish contact with them, interact with them, and enter into specific agreements lessening the economic crisis of the people. We intend to set up a common foundation for Farsi language and culture, which will address the task of teaching and research.

We assume that the conference will provide us a useful opportunity for knowing our foreign-based compatriots intimately. They too will get to know the needs and possibilities of our republic. We can benefit from their intellectual and material power to strengthen the economy and culture of our people. By remaining in isolation we cannot achieve the heights of development we have set forth for ourselves. Furthermore, we cannot find a way that takes us out of present stagnation and regress. A nation that remains in isolation is doomed.

Q: A guest is a guest, be he big or small, trader or minister. He is dear to the host. That notwithstanding, who are the outstanding personalities and known people expected to attend the conference?

A: Yes, we cannot classify guests into dear and ordinary ones. We place our house at the disposal of anybody who knocks at your door with a pure heart and pure intentions. This is truer in the case of our organization, which has invited compatriots, nationals and long distanced dear ones to be our guests. Some notable ones are Mir Muhammad Zahir Yaqubiyan, a businessman and the leader of the Tajik Union of New York, Haji Ghulam Ahmad, a Pakisani businessman, Baqir Moin, BBC staff member, Dr. Sayyad Jalal Badakhchani of The Institute of Ismaili Studies, London, and Haji Abdul Mannan Samarkandi, a businessman from Saudi Arabia who is known to your readers.

The Head of the Hamdard Institute of Pakistan, a reputed scholar and physician (of Eastern medicine) Hakim Muhammad Saeed, and the famous epigraphist Ahmad Hasan Dani, both from Pakistan, will be attending. From India Professor Nurul Hasan, the Governor of the State of West Bengal, from Afghanistan Professor Burhanu'd-Din Rabbani, Ahmad Shah Masud, General Dostum, and from Iran the President of the Islamic Republic of Iran namely Hashemi Rafsanjani, and External Affairs Minister Ali Akbar Velayati have been invited as the Guests of Honor to the conference. We have also invited official delegations from the former Soviet Republics in our neighborhood. Through their participation we intend to convey our message of fraternal and good neighborly relations to the world at large.

Q: What will be the role of political parties and organizations, factories and foundations of the Republic in the program of the conference?

A: Our first and last expectation from political parties and organizations is that they contribute to the normalization of political climate of the Republic. We request the factory and foundations and the Shirin confectionary, the Union of Karakul Preservation and the Office of Muslim *Qadis* of the Republic that each of them plays a host to the conference for one day.

Q: Is it possible for the guests to the conference to visit the families of Tajik citizens outside the frame of the scheduled program? Can only a citizen of the Republic invite them to their home as a guest?

A: Why not? Nothing forbids guests from visiting Tajik families or meeting individuals privately if they so desire. Fortunately, the days when a KGB agent shadowed a visitor are gone for good. No place is out of bonds for the guests. Likewise, any citizen of the Republic desiring to meet with any guest or inviting him to his home is free to do so. But, of course, these interactions have to be within the established norms of etiquette and morality. The World Tajik and Compatriots Abroad Conference is a historical event that has great value for the self-realization and solidarity of our people, and the future of our nation.

Interviewed by Kiranshahi Sharifzade

Seda-e Mardum, December 22,1992

From the feast of reconciliation to the stage of animation

"I pray for the comfort of all". Professor Osimi

(Interview with the Chairman of Payvand, Academician Muhammad Osimi regarding current hot stories)

Q: Professor, Sir, you have attended various meetings of the representatives of different areas in the region of Khujand, Republic of Tajikistan, and have spoken from their platform. In those meetings you have said that you believe an understanding could be forged across the board in Tajikistan.

A: Yes, I believed in that, otherwise I would not have participated in the meetings and would not have spoken there. In my speeches, I said that not only the eyes of the people of Tajikistan but also of the Tajiks world over were fixed on the conference. The participants of the World Tajik Conference held in the September of last year came to know one another through the instrumentality of the conference. They returned to their respective homes praying for the restoration of peace and security in entire Tajikistan. Our compatriots in the US, Saudi Arabia, Germany, Pakistan, Afghanistan and Iran constantly enquire of us through telephone calls, letters and telegrams about the situation in Tajikistan. They fervently hope and pray that peace and security are restored as early as possible in their beloved land and their house of hope. They expect Tajik leadership to deal with the situation wisely.

Q: Frankly speaking, there was little hope of the return of peace and security even after the re-grouping of the parliament and the sessions of the Supreme Council unless the leadership of armed groups agreed to come to the talking table. We have come to the bitter conclusion that the leaders of armed groups have better understanding and perception of the situation in comparison to the representatives of the parliament. They have also greater control over it.

A: I do not think it is so and I would not stigmatize every parliamentarian. There could be some among the representatives who are not farsighted in regard to the pending issues. But in general, they do realize their responsibilities. During the first few days of the session there was some misunderstanding among the parliamentarians. But when issues were discussed seriously and solutions sought in the right earnest, the difference melted and at this consensus of opinion was reached. Circumstances demand that we forgive and forget, and ensure that we do not land ourselves in a blind alley.

Q: It is being said that the deliberations of the Supreme Council session were abortive; the parliamentarians got bogged with the distribution of portfolios. Since you had an opportunity of attending these sessions, what impressions do you carry in regard to the issue under discussion?

A: All of us are fully aware of the difficulties we had in calling the 16th Supreme Council to session. But almost all the people's representatives attended the session despite the difficulties in their proper lodgment. In previous sessions of the Council held in normal times, attendance would not be that full. This explains that the representatives are fully conscious of their professional and civic responsibilities. For them no responsibility is greater than that of putting an end to the suicidal and fratricidal war and taking the country back to a state of normalcy. The impression that the session did not produce the desired results is based on the proceedings of its first couple of days. In my opinion the session did achieve the purpose for which it was summoned. The essential objective was to prepare the ground for interface between the peoples' deputies to the parliament from various constituencies and the leaders of armed groups. The deputies made an appeal to putting an end to the fratricidal war and restore the strife—torn country to normalcy. As regards the distribution of portfolios, about which there have been many rumours, I will say that the election of the leader of the Republic and the formation of the government is the task of the session of the Supreme Council. Our Republic has moved on to the parliamentary form of government. Therefore, implementation of what you call the "responsibility of distributing portfolios" is unavoidable. Honorable deputies have, in a unanimous decision, ousted the previous president. At the same time, they have almost unanimously elected the President of the Supreme Council, the chief of the Council of Ministers and the Ministers of the Republic. The important thing to do now is that the people of our republic, low or high, notwithstanding the place where they live or where they were born, irrespective of community affiliations and alignments to a political party or ideology, extend their support to the new leadership of Tajikistan and cooperate with it for the relief and rehabilitation of our countrymen.

Q: At the moment there is much hue and cry about the structure of the new government of Tajikistan, and the local affiliation of the members of the government. Would you like to comment on that?

A: With regard to the leadership and governmental or official duties, let us not be concerned whether the deputies are from one region or from one locality. This is not important. What is important is that in the eyes of the general public of the Republic of Tajikistan, they (those inducted into the ministries) should be capable and equipped with wisdom, sagacity competence and a sense of responsibility. They should undertake to pull Tajikistan out of economic, social, spiritual and economic crisis.

Our recently elected leadership ought to underline one fundamental objective, and that is putting an end to the fratricidal war, bringing the dispersed and absconding people back to their places of residence and providing smooth running of life. Shaykh Sa'adi says:

Adamiyyat rahm bar becharagan avardan ast
K-adami ra tan belarzad ta bebinad resh ra

Humanism means taking pity on helpless people.
For, a human being shudders on seeing a wounded fellow

Let us stop the unending debate and discussion about Tajikistan and who is holding what position. The present day Tajikistan cannot bear the burden of such discussions. A government has been elected by the people and endorsed by the Supreme Council. We should accept it and let the government perform its duties. Time will show how effectively it runs. We should respect the rule of law. At the same time, we should respect the elected members of the government. The chaos and disorder that we witness in our dear land today springs from disrespect to the law of the land.

It is sad that the forces of opposition adopted one-sided attitude in their approach towards the parliamentary debate. They confined themselves only to criticizing the government and subjecting it to great pressure. The originality and essence of opposition lies in proposing program with new dimensions, styles and patterns in place of defective plans and schemes of the government. The opposition has to be creative and work with the spirit of cooperation; if the government refuses to cooperate then it has the right to oppose.

Q: A misunderstanding has spread among the masses about the character of the opposition. They think that the opposition is anti-government. The impression is that all political parties and social and political organizations that have emerged in recent years are the creation of the opposition. Even some deputies of the parliament went to the extent of demanding that the activities of these political parties and organizations should be banned. Is such a demand justified in a democratic society that is based on the rule of law?

A: It is regrettable that it is not only the laity but also the groups of intellectuals who carry this incorrect impression. It has to be accepted that the reason for the emergence of such impressions is because of the extremism of opposition forces. You are right in your observation that in a country that adopts the rule of law as the basis of its democratic dispensation there is no reason for disallowing political parties their right to be politically active. Logic defies it. In all countries including Tajikistan political parties and social organizations have a right to their activities. But these activities have to fall within the frame of the current law and in accordance with their expressly stated statutes and manifesto. The government, in its turn, should keep its eye on the observance of the law by political and social organizations. I am not in favour of disallowing the activities of political parties and political organizations. At the same time, I oppose unbecoming activities of some of the deputies, parties and organizations.

Q: A feast for reconciliation was arranged in Khujand. It raised the hopes of the people — both high and low— of peace and order in the Republic. But soon after that strife and clashes escalated. The Khujand Feast of Reconciliation, like the Khorog truce, ended in a fiasco. How do you look at it?

A: This is a frank assessment. I, too, had great expectations from the Khujand Feast and I have not given up hope yet. The commanders of various opposing armed groups embraced one another in the presence of people and expressed their respect for the national flag by rubbing it on their eyes, stating that that was tantamount to their swearing their allegiance to it. A man cannot make a stronger show of sincerity than this in word and deed. The Supreme Council on its part promised to grant amnesty to the defaulters. Now everything depends on how sincerity the commitments and promises made are adhered to. Another aspect of the issue is that henceforth the law should have the upper hand and not the wishes or interests of the party. Anybody who confesses his sin, or commits a fresh crime after enjoying amnesty should, necessarily, be made answerable to the law of the land.

Q: Professor, Sir, towards what will the future events of the Republic gravitate: the arms wielders or the government?

A: More than anybody else, it is the government which has to be concerned with the future events, because it has been elected legally and everybody ought to accept it and show it due respect. They will have to accept whatever step the government takes. In fact they should lend their helping hand in the task of the government. It seems to me that the gun-wielding folks have also realized the disastrous consequences of in—fighting and strife. They ought to surrender their arms immediately to the government because in a society based on the rule of law arms should be with the government and not in the hands of illegal groups. At the same time, the government has to e guarantee the security of all citizens of the State.

Q: I agreed, but the procedure for surrender of arms was not defined clearly — neither in the session of the Supreme Council nor in the meeting of the commanders of militias. How do you envisage the conduct of this task?

A: The session of the Supreme Council and the meetings of the commanders of militias laid the foundation for peace in the Republic. The first step in this direction was the setting up of the Feast for Reconciliation. But many other good-will steps and initiatives have to be taken to bring about true peace and stability. Foremost of them all is putting an end to fighting in the Republic. Disarming the armed groups is essential, and this cannot be done in a day or two. It presupposes restoration of mutual confidence and a guarantee of general security to the citizens by the government. It is clear to all today that activating the forces of peace is of prime importance for Tajikistan. With their support and cooperation, it should be possible to prepare the armed groups on both sides to surrender their arms to the government. Only then can peace, order and normal life return to the war-torn country.

Q: Thank you!

Interviewed by Kiranshahi Sharif Zadeh

Celebrations: Festival within a festival

The first ten days of the month of September will witness gala celebrations in Dushanbe, the capitol of the sovereign Republic of Tajikistan. It will be recalled that these days will not only celebrate our independence but also witness the organizing of the Second Conference of World Tajik Association as well as the Second Conference of the Farsi-Tajik Language Foundation. All of us know that this grand cultural celebration is the pride not only of Tajikistan but also of our compatriots, our co-religionists and co-lingual fraternity outside the borders of Tajikistan. Our correspondent had an interview with Professor Saifu'd-Din Zadeh Osimi, the President of *Payvand* — the organization for cultural relations between Tajiks and compatriots abroad — on the preparedness and plans of holding the conference. Here we bring its excerpts to our readers:

Q: Professor, we know that celebrating the independence of the Republic of Tajikistan and the first conference of World Tajiks last year had a useful effect on the disturbed and chaotic conditions of the republic. Indeed these celebrations, though grand and unforgettable, were observed under some constraints. Now that the situation of the republic is limping back to normalcy and order is gradually restored, how will these functions proceed this year?

A: Yes, last year the Republic was in a state of turmoil and chaos. We could not celebrate the first anniversary of independence with the pomp and show that it merited. But I would be disposed to say that even in those disturbed conditions, the celebrations we held were not too bad. Perhaps these could not be better. In particular, the function of installing the statue of Abul Qasim Firdowsi, though a short one, contributed to removing animosity and estrangement from the hearts of people. It sent a message to all that the Tajiks were alert and active and would remain so.

Last year, apart from other activities, we held an international symposium on new achievements in the fields of science and culture. A large number of our co-lingual scholars participated and made seminar presentations on interesting themes.

This year, our republic is more normal than what it was. We, therefore, hope that both functions, the celebration of Independence Day and holding of the Second Forum of World Tajiks will be scaled and with a lot of fervour. This year the Organizing Committee for the celebrations has been constituted at a high level to ensure participation from the Supreme Council down to the primary schools. We are confident that these celebrations will be conducted on a grand scale with extraordinary grandeur and fervor.

Q: Who are the invitees?

A: We have invited guests from different countries of the world to the celebrations. Among them are people of our blood, faith and language, from the countries of Afghanistan, Iran, China, Hindustan, Saudi Arabia, Turkey, US and Europe. Unfortunately, our invitation reached them a bit late. In spite of that we expect that all the invitees will be with us. We have also extended invitation to the Tajiks domiciled in the Commonwealth of Independence States. We hope that the invited Tajiks from the sovereign states of Uzbekistan, Kyrgyzstan, Kazakhstan, Ukraine, Russian Federation, and Turkmenistan will arrive soon to participate in the conference.

Q: Last year only fifty per cent of the invitees attended the conference. Do you think that this year the percentage could go beyond 70 %?

A: Last year we had sent invitation letters at lest 5 – 6 months prior to the conference date. Despite that because the situation of our Republic was somewhat confusing, only half of the invitees turned up. This year it was not possible for us to send invitation letters sufficiently in advance. It is just two months to the date of holding the functions that we could send invitation letters. Well, despite all this, I am hopeful that all the invitees will make it convenient for them to participate. The situation in Tajikistan is much improved.

We are making an effort to see that delegates do attend the conference and witness the improved situation with their own eyes. Seeing is better than hearing. Once they know about the situation in our republic, they will convey it to their compatriots and friends back home that the road to visit Tajikistan is open; their security is guaranteed and they can travel without any fear. We shall have to hold consultations with them about how Tajikistan can be pulled out of economic and political crisis. We want that Tajikistan should be home of hope for the Tajiks the world over.

Q: What is the profile of the guests invited for this year's conference?

A: The invitees are essentially from the field of culture. But these also include businessmen, traders, industrialists, investors, economists and politicians. For example, among them is an American capitalist Masud Rezai. From the America-based Ya'qubi house there is Muhammad Zahir, the President of the American Association of Tajiks. This year we have invited a delegation of Israeli Tajiks too, who are from given to various professions. They can interact with their counterparts in Tajikistan, and collaborate in productive activities. Builders, technocrats, skilled workers, physicians, scholars and scientists could benefit their local counterparts; they can support one another, understand one another's thinking. The outsiders can support the insiders by jointly setting up factories and initiating the process of conducting business.

In short, as I said earlier the basic purpose of this year's World Conference of Tajiks is to provide opportunity for consultations focused on finding ways and means of pulling the Tajikistan out of its economic and political crisis.

Q: Holding of independence celebrations and organizing Second Tajik International entail considerable expenditure. Is Payvand meeting all the expenses or is the government meeting a part of the expenses?

A: We hope that our patrons will meet the cost of the inaugural function. We have already declared our bank balance. The Organizing Committee is hopeful that factories, foundations, organizations, companies and citizens with conscience and a spirit of nationalism will make their contribution and support our invitation with all the warmth of their hearts. At no time and in no conditions have the

Tajiks forsaken their characteristic role of playing a very cordial host to guests? Of course, the Supreme Council and the government have made commitment to underwrite part of the expenditure.

Q: For the first time after a thousand years from the days of Samanid kingdom, the Tajiks came together last year, talked to one another, deliberated over many issues and then dispersed. What was their experience from that conclave?

A: The people of the country established contact with the Tajiks from outside the country. This could not have materialized without the instrumentality of *Payvand*. It is indeed a big achievement for the Tajiks, wherever they are. What is more important than this is that we got the opportunity just came to know them and now we can reach them without an intermediary, and whenever we so desire.

Q: You are an expert on Farsi language. In what state do you find it at the moment and what are your comments on Farsi-Tajiki?

A: I would like to say with all humility that for over half a century I have been struggling to obtain the status of an official language for Farsi. I was one of the foremost advocates of introducing Farsi books in the curriculum of Secondary and Higher Secondary Schools. During my tenure as the Principal of Polytechnic College, I introduced Farsi as the medium of instruction in the first and the second year. It was difficult in the beginning but we succeeded in the end.

Q: Perhaps there was opposition to this measure from the higher authorities and it was disallowed?

A: No, the leadership of the day did not know about it, or may be they did, but it did not make it an issue. Students and teachers welcomed it. At the end of the day, it became a part of the tradition and imparting lessons to the students at higher levels in Tajiki was also introduced, and continues till today.

The language bill was passed in the Central Committee and then the Academy of Sciences of Tajikistan endorsed it. That is the basis for obtaining official status. Then I became the Vice President of the draft committee for drafting the law pertaining to language. The law that we accepted for giving the language official status was a people friendly law. Raising it to the status of an official language was not to undermine the other languages of the republic. In fact these languages such as Uzbek, Russian, and Kyrgyz are freely used.

Implementing the law about language, that too within a specific time, is impossible under the present circumstances. With a fratricidal war and economic crisis it is not possible to promulgate such a law. But this does not mean that we abandon the effort. However, apart from this, the state of our education and training, too, is not good. In order to be a linguist, the knowledge of language is not enough. One should have the ability of cultivating language. We should popularize the spoken language. We should also pay full attention to the method of teaching the prescribed books. Above all, our students should develop the culture of reading books. Only then can we preserve our simple, and enervating language. I must add that passing of the language bill also contributes to national solidarity.

Q: Next year *Shahnameh* celebrations would be added to the three functions. How is *Payvand* geared up to this task?

A: The Tajiks were the main initiators of the Millennium celebrations of *Shahnameh*. Next year, these celebrations will be held from September 5 to 10 along with the Tajik International. We are gearing up to this function right now. We shall be inviting famous *Shahnameh* experts from all over the world. We are eager that intellectuals, scholars, poets, writers, teachers, and students should participate in this celebration. In this context I would like to state that the media should be active. We would like that during the coming year we organize competition of *Shahnameh* recitation and encourage the winners by giving them awards. The competition should take place at the foot of the statute of Firdowsi. At that site, we should also set up a *Shahnameh* Exhibition, and *Shahnameh* recitation should thus become the part of our tradition. We should bring to life Ajam at that very ground.[2]

Q: What do you wish for the guests, the participants of Second Tajik International and the delegates to the celebrations of Tajikistan's Independence Day?

A: I welcome them with a smiling face and with immense pleasure. I wish them happiness in the land of Tajiks, as this is their own home, the land of their ancestors. This is their festival and our festival.

Q: Thanks for the interview

Interviewed by Azim Khan Niyaz

Nidoi Ranjbar September 3,1993

Tajikistan is the House of Hope for Tajiks all Over the World

These days, people of all ages in the length and breadth of the country are gearing up for celebrating Tajikistan's Second Anniversary of independence and the Second Forum of Tajiks from all over the world.

For obtaining fuller detail about preparations for celebrating the functions, we have with us Professor Muhammad Osimi, President of the Payvand Organzation.

Q: Professor, may we begin with congratulating you for setting afoot preparations for these celebrations.

A: Thank you!

Q: One of the upcoming celebrations relates to the Independence of Tajikistan. If we did not have independence until now, does that mean that the October Revolution did not give us our independence?

A: I have made several statements on television stating that I consider the Tajiks themselves governed the Republic for last 70 years. In other words, our self-governance began in 1924. Our independence actually began with the formation of our Republic. However, this independence was relative, because we were dependent on Moscow. Now it has been two years that our Republic is completely independent. However, full independence will take its time to shape. Indeed, it's been two years that our leadership has been able to act independently. Today, we are a sovereign nation with a free hand. More than one hundred countries throughout the world have recognized our independence.

Q: Talking about preparations, what are its broad outlines? How does this year's Forum for All Tajiks differ from the previous year?

A: I would like to say that the First Forum was well prepared and successfully brought to completion. We had much time to make preparations for it. The main difference between the two is that the First Forum was created on the initiative of Payvand, an organization for cultural relations of Tajik compatriots abroad. The second forum was initiated by the Supreme Parliament of the Republic. All of us are aware that this year a high level Committee for the Preparation of the Celebrations is constituted with the President of the Republic, Immomali Rahmon as its chairman. I would like to mention that the organizational assignment of these preparations has been given to Payvand, the Association of Friendship, the Ministry of Culture and the Ministry of Foreign Affairs.

It should be mentioned that according to the regulations of our Association, the World Forum of Tajiks should be held once every three years.

This year's celebration has an additional purpose. It is very timely because our compatriots will be coming together at a time when foreign media outlets are relentless in spreading many false stories against us. Let our guests come to Tajikistan and see with their own eyes. They can tell the world what are the plans of the Government of Tajikistan, and what it is doing for the people of the country.

Q: Where are the invitees from?

A: They are from sixteen foreign countries besides from all of the former Soviet Republics, with the exception of the Baltic States. However, I would like to mention that there are many difficulties of travel these days. There are many willing participants, but it is difficult for them to come. For example, to come from Pakistan through Tashkent, air ticket is sold out a month in advance. We very much want that all participants are able to attend the celebrations and the Forum.

Q: As you indicated, the Government of the Republic will meet all expenses for the celebration. Are there any other sources of funding?

A: Of course, we have prompted all involved ministries and institutions to be partners in fundraising activities such as concerts and lotteries. This would support the Forum.

Q: What is the program for celebrating the second anniversary of the independence of the Republic of Tajikistan's and the Second Forum of Tajiks world over?

A: The guests will start arriving in Dushanbe on September 5th. They will stay in the Republic until the 13th of September. First, they will be taken on a sightseeing tour of the capital of Tajikistan. Then, they will participate in wreath laying ceremony at the statues of great Tajik celebrities like Abu Abdallah Rudaki, Abu Ali ibn-i Sina, Abu'l Qqsim Firdowsi, Sadr'ad-Din Aini, Mirzo Tursunzodah, Bobojon Gafurov and others. The opening ceremony of the World Forum of Tajiks will take place on the 8th of

September, which will be followed by a press conference. In the morning of September 9, there will be a national celebration on the main streets of Tajikistan where people will gather together and celebrate Independence Day of the Republic. The main ceremony marking the Independence Day will take place from 3 pm to 5.30 pm at the Stadium Frunze. The President of Tajikistan, Rahmonov will felicitate the guests and the citizens of the Republic. Then the festivities will begin. From 10 to 11 of September, the guests will tour other towns and villages of Tajikistan. On the 12th of September, there will be a closing press conference in the small hall of the Ministries for summarizing the events.

Q: The last question: Professor, the celebration of the 1,000 year of the Shahnameh of Firdowsi is scheduled to take place next year. What are Paywand's preparations for it?

A: Good you asked me that question. We the Tajiks are the main initiators of celebrations marking the millennium of the philosopher-poet Firdowsi and his epic Shahnameh. Fortunately, the celebrations will be held from the 5th to the 10th of September of next year. Preparations are well underway, and *inshaallah*, celebrations will be a success. Renowned Shahnameh experts will participate in the celebrations. A good number of scholars, poets, writers and others will also be invited.

Thank you for your informative and thought provoking conversation.
Interviewed by Umari Sherkhon
English translation by Sitora Rashidova – granddaughter of M.Osimi

---

Dushanbe, Tajikistan, 1995

Art and Science in the 21st Century

by Muhammad Osimi

The 21st century of the Greenwich calendar is coming to a conclusion. The transition from the 20th century into the 21st is a unique milestone in humanity's history. On the eve of this occasion, people are reflecting on the fates of humanity. What will the world be like in the 21st century? What will the relations between nations and states look like? Will the spirit of mutual understanding and mutual tolerance finally reign the world, and will people of different nations and different beliefs live together in harmony? Or will discord and intolerance continue to bring endless calamities as before? These questions trouble the intellectuals of East and West. Today, the greatest responsibility of the intellectual community lies in uniting people closer together; to bring forces together to in the fight against intolerance.

In July of 1995, in the capital of Georgia, Tbilisi, the International Forum, "For Solidarity, Against Intolerance? For a dialogue of Culture" took place. In the working paper of the forum, a detailed analysis of the roots of intolerance and hatred between nations was provided.

Participants of the forum highlighted the necessity of dialogue between cultures as a method of overcoming hostility between nations.

Art and science remain important factors in bringing mutual understanding and harmony among people.

It is known that science in itself is universal. Science is the result of the efforts of some of humanity's brightest minds, and thus belongs to all of humanity. This applies to all periods of scientific development: from mythological ideas to the greatest modern inventions. Science cannot be forced under a nationalistic frame, nor can it be divided between East and West.

Looking over the historical past, one can observe geographical shifts in the scientific epicenters throughout the world. China, Egypt, India, Mesopotamia, and then Greece were the ancient centers of scientific thought. In the middle ages, science was successfully developing in the Islamic world. In the new and newer times, Europe became the center of scientific progress. As the centers shifted, a sense of continuity prevailed. Efforts of the scientists who came before, were strengthened by those who came after. In the new scientific centers, a synthesis of scientific achievements of different countries and nations would take place, and on this basis further progress was achieved. This phenomenon can be observed in any sphere of knowledge.

Let's take for example, medicine. First records of medicinal knowledge took place in the ancient cradles of human civilization: China, Egypt, Mesopotamia, and Iran. This knowledge was then absorbed in Greece and what is now known as Greek Medicine formed (Tibbi Yunoni).

This medicine became the achievement of the Islamic world and received further strengthened development because of the efforts of Arabic and Iranian scholars, first of all Abu-Bakr Razi (Rasis) and Abu Ali Ibn Sina or Avicenna. As the saying goes, if the basis of medicinal science was created by Galen and Hippocrates, then they were perfected by Rasis and Avicenna.

The same can be said of many other subjects, astronomy, trigonometry, algebra, chemistry.

In more modern times, Europe has been the current gatekeeper of scientific and technological progress. This is the strength of Western power. This fact was even highlighted by Muhammad Iqbal. However, beginning with the late 20th century, the countries of the East also became more and more prominent in the scientific orbit, Japan, China, India, Pakistan, republics of Central Asia, etc. Some countries of the East have surpassed the West in their technological advancements; take for example, Japan and its electronics industry.

The 21st century should be the century of technological globalization. In the coming years, scientific knowledge should be the wealth of all nations of our planet.

As a result, it will be necessary to review the secondary and tertiary educational systems and create the necessary conditions to attract talented youth to the scientific realm. In this regard, the charitable initiative to create schools for gifted children in Pakistan, Hamdard, headed by Hakim Muhammad Said, deserves much praise.

In the 21st century, it will be imperative to harness scientific progress for the common good. Scientific progress must serve for the benefit of people. This is a truth, one that is often repeated by scientists. However, we continue to witness the use of scientific achievements in the interest of war and methods of mass destruction. The scientific community must come together in solidarity in order to prevent science from being used in a way that is harmful to humanity.

Another important factor responsible for bringing people together is art. Art, in contrast from science has its own specificity. Each nation has its own musical traditions and one is taught from childhood to appreciate and enjoy its music, with its own national purposes. Learning to enjoy one's own music from an early age, also leads one to be able to appreciate the musical traditions of other nations.

Modern methods of communication: radio, television, film, serve as channels that spread different musical cultures. In the 21st century methods of communication will be even stronger, making the nations of all continents neighbors.

In this aspect, I would like to draw attention to the widespread popularity of the musical culture of the West in the countries of the East. It is known that in the West there exists a high humanitarian culture and a mass popular culture. Unfortunately, the youth finds itself more attracted to the latter because it is more accessible. For growing an appreciation for high culture requires proper education and a proper upbringing. For example, pop music is quickly absorbed by youth, but the timeless classical masterpieces of music belonging to the likes of Beethoven, Mozart, Tchaikovsky, Verdi and others, are not as easily accepted by youth without a proper prior education. Consequently, in order to avoid the pitfalls of substandard music of the West, it is necessary cultivate an appreciation for the higher arts at an early age.

We often speak about the cultural expansion of the West, and even of cultural colonialism. However, we forget that the people of Western nations themselves are affected by the pestilent influences of the so-called mass produced music.

The best musical works of Western culture are not alien to the East, as reaching the people of the East can also be part of the wealth of the West.

In the future, interaction and mutual influence of cultures will continue to intensify. And concurrently, a synthesis of cultures will also begin to take place, which will serve the noble cause of bringing nations together.

English translation by Sitora Rashidova – granddaughter of M.Osimi

———————————————

We have come from ages...

(The last meeting with Professor Osimi)

In Dushanbe, the capital of Tajikistan, Tajiks from outside its borders meet once a year, and get an opportunity to meet with their acquaintances and friends. The initiator and ambassador of this mission was the grand old wise man who made strenuous efforts for the unity and solidarity of the nation. The outstanding Tajik scholar, Academic of the Academy of Sciences of Tajikistan, the President of the Payvand organization, Vice President of the World Association of Tajiks and the President of International Organization of Central Asian Cultural Studies, has demonstrated in his scientific and historical writings that the Tajik-Farsi speaking peoples have a history and civilization that goes back to thousands of years.

Professor Muhammad Osimi had all along nursed a desire to witness the unity, prosperity, security and progress of the people of his country. Shamsu'd-Din Shaheen has very rightly said:

Labat be khandeh faraham shaved bedan khubi
Kih barg-i laleh be barg-e digar dehi Payvand
The smile binds your lips with a beauty
That the petal of tulip gets attached to other petal

It is sad that the arrow of ignorance pierced his warmly vibrant heart.[3] This brutality has been condemned by the Tajik society as well as the world at large. In a statement the President of the Association of International Relations of Farsi Speaking Peoples of the World, namely Payvand, this has been labeled as a satanic act.

Great men are like angels. Despite his wisdom and the status of a patriarch, he was humble and sensitive. Only four days before the tragic event of his assassination, the chief editor of the weekly *Adabiyyat wa San'at*, Gulnazar, the poet, called me to her presence and said that Professor Osimi had just returned from Paris with a very valuable work, the third volume of *The History of Central Asian Civilization* titled 'The Highway of Knowledge'. It would be in the fitness of things if we could arrange a meeting with him to put forth our proposal for publishing this invaluable work, and also discuss the preliminaries for the celebration of the fifth anniversary of the independence of our Republic and an international symposium of World Tajiks. I thought this a good idea and proceeded towards the work place of Professor Osimi. His office was packed with visitors. I waited in the corridor. When the visitors left after a while, I sought permission to enter. He was in high spirits and excited to see me. He enquired about my welfare and then beckoned me to take a seat. Perhaps he had understood the purpose of my visit as he pulled out a book from his drawer. Holding it in his hand, he joyfully said to me, "*The History of Central Asian Civilization* Volume III." I almost snatched the book from his hands. This volume with the sub-heading *The Highway of Civilization* was in English language with an excellent get up. It carried the Foreword by Muhammad Osimi. I expressed my very warm congratulations to Professor Osimi for this rare and valuable volume. Then I told him the purpose for which I had come to see him.

In a very sweet voice, the Professor began, "Very well, my son, it is a noble act to acquaint our people with this valuable treasure. I would like to talk on this subject tomorrow because I have a lot of work to do and if we continue our conversation, it would not be to our satisfaction. If you wish it I can come to see you tomorrow."

The next day, at the appointed time, Professor Osimi presented himself at the office of the chief editor of *The Weekly*. We once again congratulated him on the publication of this volume. He thanked us and said that it was not an easy task to publish this invaluable scientific and cultural work. Eminent scholars from near and far off countries and our own scholars have rendered untiring service, and he himself worked for one long year as the head of the board of editors. He said that at the UN organization some people created obstructions in their work but because he happened to be the head of the board, they could not have their way.

After a pause, Professor Osimi continued," Now after completing this assignment several other tasks await our attention. If luck favors and security and peace return to our Republic, we may be able to bring these tasks to completion."

His bright face turned slightly pale. Gulnazar handed him a cup of tea and said, "Professor, you are the support and source of inspiration for all Tajik intellectuals, and we hope that you will bring more fresh treasures to the fund of Tajik sciences and culture." Professor Osimi smiled and poignantly said, "I earnestly desire that our people who have gone through hardships and privation return to their native land. Friendship and fraternal sentiments, unity and mutual understanding would bring stability to our small nation. Maybe once again I get the opportunity of sitting together with my students, colleagues, friends and common people and speaking about peace and reconciliation.

This was our last meeting with professor Muhammad Osimi. This was the last moment his words rang in our ears. This was the last moment when we benefited from his kindness and courtesy. Live long in memory, O you self-consuming seer!

Dear readers, here we bring to you our last meeting with Professor Muhammad Osimi.

The self-Recognition of a nation stems from projecting self.

Q: Readying a valuable work for printing is in reality a new and proud opening for the Tajik nation and Tajikistan. Through this invaluable treasure, the people will establish their right they deserved. On behalf of the entire Tajik nation and the readership of the weekly *Adabiyyat wa San'at*, we once again congratulate you on having taken great pains in compiling this volume that brings self-recognition to our nation. Would you kindly help us identify of Central Asia?

A: Yes, before everything else, we should clarify the meaning of Central Asia. Like several entities, the Central Asia too has had changes. It has geographical, political, historical, cultural and administrative aspects. When we speak of the history of Central Asian civilization, we usually focus on the historical and cultural aspects of the region. In some eras of their history, Central Asians were able to raise large empires and powerful centralized governments like the Empires of the Achaemenians, Alexander of Macedonia, Kushanas, Samanids, Timur, and Timurid. Thus when on the prompting of Bobojon Ghafurov we started learning the history of Central Asia, UNESCO accepted the meaning of Central Asia in the same sense viz, historical and cultural. On that basis, the organization of the Studies in Central Asian Civilization included these countries: erstwhile Republics of Soviet Central Asia, Kazakhstan, Afghanistan, Iran, Pakistan, Western China and Mongolia. The aforementioned organization had been incepted in 1973 as a result of the initiative of Bobojon Gafurov. He was its first president. Now I am the Head of this organization.

Q: Who undertook the publishing of this valuable work? Kindly tell us about its theme and contents for the benefit of our readers.

A: The organization for the Study of Central Asian Civilization had proposed History *of Central Asian Civilization* in six volumes. UNESCO endorsed the proposal, and thereafter, an International Scientific Committee was constituted to pursue the project. The Committee drew the timeframe as follows: Volume I, *The Beginning of Civilization*, covers the period from ancient times to 7 B.C. This volume in English was brought out under the editorship of two scholars, Ahmad Dani from Pakistan and Masson from Russia. The volume begins with Civilization *is the First Bridge* by Ranov, a member of the Academy of Sciences of Tajikistan. He has made a painstaking study of Tajikistan. Excavations in the village Tut Quwul of Hisar revealed to him the existence of habitats of primitive man at that site. Stone tools of that civilization have proved this. People all over the world will get acquainted with his findings through this book and, naturally, they will come to know of the civilization in Hisar. The author has dealt with all the three stages of Stone Age, Bronze Age and Iron Age. Famous scholars, Professor Thapar (India), Dani (Pakistan), Joyandeh (Afghanistan) and Ahmad Ali of Uzbekistan have compiled the history of the peoples of Central Asia during these periods.

The Hungarian scholar Harmata Bussy has written an insightful research paper regarding the origin of the Indo-European tribes in Central Asia. He has revised the opinion about the migration of Aryan communities. Up to this day, the common belief was that the Aryans had come to the Central Asian region around the second millennium B.C. But he has presented an array of arguments to assert that the Aryan tribes had begun to migrate to Central Asia in the fourth millennium B.C, culminating in their mass migration in the second millennium B.C. Professor Harmata has listed positive factors that indicate the movement of Aryans from one place to another. In this context, he gives importance first of all to the horse, and horse driven two—wheeled or four—wheel chariots. There is detailed and convincing presentation on the importance of Amu (Oxus) and Syr (Jaxartes) valleys where the early Aryan tribes had settled down. Professor Litvinsky, Joyandeh and Nigorov have richly contributed to this section.

From a study of the first volume of the work, a reader can conclude that the Aryan tribes had settled down in Central Asia over a period of several millennia and continued to live there.

Volume II of the work, *Exploration of Urban and Nomadic Civilizations* covers the period from 7th century B.C. up to 250 A.D. This was the period of the Achaemenian, the Graeco-Bactrian, the Kushanian and the beginning of the Sassanian Empire. Outstanding scholars who have contributed to this chapter are B.A Litvinsky, T.A. Pugachenkova, Ysupov and Muhammadjanov (Uzbekistan), Dandakayov (Kazakhstan), Koreah N (Pakistan), Husayn Shah (Afghanistan), Reza Shahbani (Iran), Dani (Pakistan), Bernard (France) and Numan Nematov of Tajikistan.

The chapter dealing with the founding of the Greco-Bactrian Empire — one that directly concerns the ancestors of Tajiks — is of great significance. We know that Alexander the Great defeated the Achaemenian king and seized Central Asia, and the Greco-Bactrian Empire came into being. Bobojon Ghafurov writes, "Although sometime occupation of a region leads to destruction and massacre of indigenous people, it also leads to the fusion of civilizations. Interaction and mutual impact of cultures ensues". This precisely happened in Central Asia. The Greeks brought not only into the region but also accepted facets of indigenous civilization. This makes their civilization an amalgam of the Eastern and Western civilizations.

An interesting and illuminating chapter in this volume deals with the Kushans. One may say that it was Bobojon Ghafurov who attracted the attention of historians and antiquarians to explore the civilization of Kushanian period. The UNESCO organized an international conference in Dushanbe in 1968 for the study of Kushanian civilization. Several outstanding scholars of ancient history like Girshman, Bernard, Gory, Dani and Richard Fry shed fresh light on many hitherto unknown mysteries of the period. The conference established that the period of Kushans was the golden period of Central Asia. This theme has been elaborately discussed in the volume under review with special reference to items such as economic and political life, town planning, language and script.

A chapter titled 'North Western Empire of Central Asia' has been contributed by the Tajik scholar Numan Nematov, who has focused his research on the region lying between Aral Sea, Amu Darya and Syr Darya. While discussing the governance of this region, he describes with careful and scholarly detail the coming into being of the cities of Khwarazm, Ferghana Valley, Khujand, Istaravshan, Chirchek, Ahangaran, Sham and others. Apart from this, he has also analyzed the ethnic factor to prove that at that period of history, the ancestors of the present—day Tajiks occupied the land. He contends that the presumption of Northern Turkic tribes settling down in this region is untenable on the basis of irrefutable evidence. The themes like the coming up of towns, town planning, agricultural pursuits based on irrigation system are all of great significance. He has tried to show that in those days minerals were obtained from the mines in Kara Mazar, Maskan, Kani-i Mansur and Ahangaran. We know these names even today.

In this period the Silk Route that linked the East with the West had developed extensively for the transmission of trade and culture. It passed through historical cities of Central Asia like Balkh, Khatlan, Bukhara, Samarkand and Khujand. This highway was a conduit not only for transporting of commodities but also transporting of scientific, cultural and religious ideas. The teachings of the Buddha reached China and Japan through the same route. It also brought the religion of Sun Worship and of Manicheans from Central Asia to Europe. Researches have established that Sogdians played an important role along the Silk Route. Sogdian was the only language used by the traders running this highway. The lands stretching from South Korea to the shores of the Mediterranean Sea were the habitat of the Sogdian people who were active along the Silk route.

Prof. Dani has found more than a thousand stone inscriptions, most of them in Sogdian language, along the Karakorum Highway. One of these bears the name and picture of a youth of Penjikent.

Volume III of the compendium begins with the Sassanian Empire of Iran, which finds full expansion in Volume III. Volume II bearing the title *The Highway of Civilization* covers the period from A.D. 250 to A.D. 750. It deals exhaustively with the Sassanians of Iran and also the language and civilization in that period. 'The Kingdom of Khwarazm' by Bolganov is also mentioned in it. Nematov and Marshak have contributed their researches on the Kingdom of the Sogds. The volume ends with the conquest of the Arabs by Abdul Hamid Jalilov, Litvinsky and Kolesnikov. Exquisite illustrations make it highly attractive. The photographs of coins and numismatic fund bring the history to life.

Volume IV encompasses the second half of the 15th century of *The History of Central Asian Civilization*. Professor Bosfor and I were assigned the task of compiling this section. We gave it the title of 'The Period of Revival'. In fact this is the period of revival of Ajam (Iran). Since the historical material designed to fill this volume was vast and copious, I approached the International Committee with the suggestion that we divide the material into two parts. Part I would comprise history, society and economy, and Part II would deal with the development of science and culture. Both parts are now ready for printing. Tajik scholars have worked laboriously to compile separate chapters of the volume. Nematov wrote the chapter dealing with the era of Somonids, Kapranov wrote the chapter on linguistics, Dinarshayov wrote the chapter on philosophy and Muqaddam Ashrafi wrote the chapter on miniature work. I had to write extensively for this chapter.

Volumes V and VI are getting ready for printing. These volumes require invaluable services of eminent Tajik scholars and historians like Iskandarov and Mukhtarov. As has already been said, this work has to be in English language. Scholars all over the world have rated the first volume very high. Large orders were placed for quick shipment, and as such we decided to bring out its second edition.

Our co-professionals in Iran have started its translation into Farsi, and we are hopeful that soon this invaluable treasure of knowledge will come to the hands of Tajik readers.

A heart reaches the heart...

Q: Members of our society will be celebrating the fifth anniversary of Tajikistan's independence. Fortunately the Tajik International will also be held for the third time in Dushanbe at the same time. May I request you to tell us what steps *Payvand* has taken during these five years for the expansion of science and culture and for strengthening friendship with our fraternity abroad? What are the plans of *Payvand* for holding the function regularly in future?

A: Let me say that the first conference of Tajik International was simultaneously with the first anniversary of Tajik republic's independence. In the first conclave, compatriots from different countries of the world, Europe, USA, Saudi Arabia, Pakistan and in particular Iran and Afghanistan participated. That was a grand and imposing conclave although the country at that time was caught in internal dissensions and strife. Our hope that the conclave would help reduce the turmoil in the country. Our expectations came true, and precisely that happened. Our guests proceeded to the Badakhshan Mountain, the suburbs of Kulab and to Qurgan Teppeh where the local population received them — their compatriots — with warmth and smiles. Our compatriots abroad expressed their thanks to the organizers of the conclave and the *Payvand* earned the title *Kanun wa Anjuman-e Tajikan.*

Let me recount that one particular event has left an indelible impression on me: that is the unveiling of the statue of the great sage and savant Firdowsi. International press quickly disseminated the news, which reached the Farsi-Tajik speaking peoples of the world. I was in Los Angeles where many of my compatriots asked me about the statue of Firdowsi. They said that in truth Tajikistan was proud to make such a remarkable contribution to Farsi-Tajik literature and to its poetry of universal appeal. Great intellectuals like Rudaki, Firdowsi, Nasir Khusrav, Khayyam, Hafiz, Sa'adi, Kamal, Bedil, Maulana Rumi, Jami and others, all have, through their words of wisdom, united the hearts of the peoples of the orient, particularly of the Farsi-Tajik speaking humanity.

In 1993, the Second Tajik International was held in the wake of the second year of Tajikistan's independence. A group of our compatriots and co-linguists, who had already participated in the first conclave, got the opportunity of coming to Tajikistan again. It reflected their extraordinary regard and love for our people and land. The President of our Republic, Imamali Rahmanov, was elected President of World Tajik Association. Two years have passed by. During third conclave of World Tajik Association, a conference on the *Shahnameh* Millennium was held and in the fourth independence anniversary, a commemorative function for the famous saint Mir Sayyid 'Ali Hamadani was organized with all pomp and splendor. We intend to organize the third conclave of the World Tajik Association along with the fifth anniversary of Tajik independence.

A close look will show that holding a massive cultural conclave simultaneously with the Independence Day celebration will awaken our nation to its cultural heritage. Today national pride is one of the fundamental bases. We are hopeful that the third conclave will lead us towards that objective.

Now to the question of the activities of Payvand during the period between the two conclaves: the objective of Payvand is to expand cultural relations of our country with our fraternity living outside its borders. We are in direct contact with friends with whom we cultivated acquaintance during the first and the second conclaves. Our friends too have played their part in expanding cultural relations in the countries where they reside.

Dr. Sayyad Jalal Badakhchani has founded the European chapter of Payvand in London. Its aim is to collect material and secure support for Tajikistan. He has made efforts to persuade the authorities to establish the air link between London and Dushanbe. He has also prompted British investors to invest in Tajikistan, especially for the exploration of oil in Tajikistan.

Tajik Cultural Relations Association under the name of Rudaki has been established in Paris. Its chief, Masud Mirshahi, is a physician by profession but keenly interested in literature. He is very active in expanding the activities of the organization. He wants that international conferences be organized in Tajikistan and that a direct link between the universities in Paris and in Tajikistan, particularly with the Avicenna Medical Institute in Paris, is established.

Pamir Research Institute has benefited immensely from the efforts of this noble person. He endeavors to promote tourism in Tajikistan. World Tajik Association has also been incepted in America. It is headed by a businessman Muhammad Zahir Ya'qubi. Reza Moini heads the Los Angeles branch of *Payvand*. The first step, which his branch took in expanding cultural relations, was to arrange a visit of the reputed Iranian artists Sattar to our country. He is determined to provide all possible help for developing cultural relations between Farsi – Tajik speaking people of California with Tajikistan. I may add that Farsi-Tajik speaking people of California evince keen interest in our country.

The branches of *Payvand* in Pakistan and Afghanistan are also active. In the case of Afghanistan, the representatives of the branch works in close collaboration with the local government in the task of sending back the people of our Republic who were forced to go into exile. In recent years, cultural relations between Tajikistan and Iran have expanded fairly and *Payvand* is really thankful to Iran. I have great pleasure in extending my thanks to Shabistari, His Excellency the Iranian Ambassador in Tajikistan. He looked to the participation of influential delegation in all activities preceding the holding of independence anniversary celebrations. We are hopeful that a good number of scholars and littérateurs will participate in the commemorative celebrations of Kamal Khujandi. The third conclave will be started in accordance with the instructions from the President, Imamali Rahmanov. The organizing committee has expressed its all round preparedness for this event. In collaboration with the Academy of Sciences of Tajikistan, Union of Writers and the Ministry of External Affairs, *Payvand* has prepared a list of the invitees to this conference. I expect more than 220 of our compatriots and co-linguists to participate in this function and add to its splendor and dignity.

We crave for quick return of peace and amity in our dear country. We want that our compatriots who were forced by circumstances to leave their native land, return to their homes and rehabilitate themselves and help bring Tajikistan back to its glory and prosperity.

Compiled by Sunnatullah Abdullah.

———————————————

Qaraqum July 11,1996

Interview with the Correspondents of Television Sogd

Q: Professor Osimi, Sir, the people of Tajikistan are poised to hold three big and important functions simultaneously: Independence Day celebrations, Third Forum of Tajiks all over the world and Commemorative function of Kamal of Khujand. We would be glad to have your comment on this event.

A: Thanks. First of all let me thank you for giving me an opportunity of talking face to face with my compatriots through the medium of television. I send them good wishes. It should be possible to sum up the purpose of these three functions in one word, 'national pride' In these destiny—shaping days of our nation, days of great hardships for the people of Tajikistan, the importance of national pride and dignity is extraordinarily enormous. I consider national dignity a very important and strong instrument for forging national unity and solidarity. If we the Tajiks understand who we are, who we were, what we possessed and what opportunity we had grabbed in the course of human history to specify our status, we shall be able to realize the value of our new found country and we shall be able to appreciate the richness of our dear native land. Once that happens, we shall forget our senseless dissensions: we will work for the rehabilitation of our country and for the welfare of our people.

I have said it already; these three functions are interlinked and finally converge in our national pride. Tajikistan is now independent. But we have not as yet understood this as we should. We have not, as yet, distanced ourselves from the tendency of alignment (with a big power).We still think that our country is aligned (as a federating unit *tr*). Independence means to act with a sense of responsibility, to build our house with our own hands and with our own labor. We should not pin hopes on others; we should try to repair what is broken and damaged on our own and we should care for our future. We must ensure our country's territorial integrity, national solidarity and the unity among the people. We need to understand that Tajikistan does not mean only the government; it is the people of this land. Tajikistan is the house of hope for all Tajiks of the world. It is the home of hope for all the Tajiks who are scattered all over the world. Fate has been cruel to us the Tajiks as it scattered us all over the globe. They can be welded into one unit only by self-realization, self – estimation and national pride. We at the *Payvand* work towards this end and the President of our Republic lent us his helping hand. It is because of this support that we contemplate calling the World Tajik Convention one again simultaneously with the Independence Day celebrations. You may recollect that the first Tajik International was held in the first anniversary of our Independence Day and the second in the second anniversary. In the third independence anniversary, we had a conference, which testified to our national pride. It was the millennium celebration of immortal *Shahnameh* of Firdowsi. The fourth congress was also as grand as the previous one. We commemorated Mir Sayyid Ali Hamadani, the outstanding saint of the East, along with the fourth year of independence celebrations. Now that the fifth year of our independence celebrations is round the corner, we are preparing to organize the Third Tajik International to commemorate Khwajeh Kamal of Khujandi.

The credit of introducing his native land to the world at large goes to Khwajeh Kamal. When we speak of Shiraz, our mind immediately goes to Khwajeh Hafiz and Sa'adi. These two celebrated poets have invoked a special type of attachment and love of the people of the world for Shiraz. When you talk of Shiraz, you talk of flowers; when you talk of Shiraz, your lips taste sweet. The name of this city brings to you an amalgam of poetry and music. In the same way when you talk of Khwajeh Kamal, it brings to your mind the city of Khujand, and when you talk of Khujand it reminds you of Khwajeh Kamal. People of the world show respect to Khujand because of Khwajah Kamal. An Iranian poetess Turan Shahriyari sent me her verses yesterday. These refer to Kamal and its closing verse is:

Khujandi javidan bada Khujandat
Dil-e ahl-e adab shud paybandat

Oh ye from Khujand ! let Khujand be immortal for you
The hearts of men of letters remain enslaved to you

Khujand has chained the hearts of men of letters like the illustrious Kamal, Mahasti Khujandi, Abu Mahmud Khujandi, and Tash Khwajah Asiri. And this function is organized with the clear intention of arousing the sense of national pride of the Tajiks and their compatriots abroad. One who lives in Tajikistan ought to have the sharp sense of national pride because Tajikistan is his native land and he should be proud of it. Tajikistan has opened its bosom to him. That is the reason why we invited our compatriots from abroad. Now the question is how are we preparing ourselves for the event and how are our preparations?

I shall not speak about the organizing committee because its first meeting with the President of the Republic, Imamali Sharifovich Rahmanov in the chair, took place in Khujand only yesterday. Preparations for the event were discussed in detail. I shall speak about the duties assigned to me. This pertains to sending invitations to our guests. I have already said that the job of drawing the list of invitees has been entrusted to the External Affairs Ministry, Academy of Sciences and the Union of Writers at the *Payvand*. We fixed the number of invitees at 200 and they come from different parts of the world.

Q: Professor, could you please tell us from which countries are they drawn?

A: To begin with, I should mention Kamal Khujandi's second home, and that is Iran. May I help you to remember what Kamal had said about himself: that he was born in Khujand and reached the heights of fame as a poet there but spent more than half of his life in Tabriz where he lies buried. Therefore, Iran is his second home. He has said:

Tabriz mara ba ja-e jan khwahad bud
Payvasteh mara wird-e zaban khwhad bud

Tabriz is dear to me like my own life
Its name will always be on my tongue

Although he was staying in Tabriz, he missed Khujand.
When he was a prisoner of Tokhtamish, he said:

Bigzar ba Khujand, Biguh ba yoron
Az man, ki asiri shahri chinam

May be some fruits were brought from Khujand, to Tabriz, which made him say:

Mewah-e kaz Khujand mi arand
Anchunan abdar wa shirin ast

Fruits that are brought from Khujand
Are so juicy and sweet

He longed for the sweet fruits of Khujand.

From Iran we have invited many scholars who have had specialized on Kamal. One among them was Iraj Gulsurkhi who has rendered meritorious service to Farsi-Tajik literature. He published the *Diwan* of Kamal in two volumes with a detailed Introduction from his pen. We may not agree with all that he has stated in the introduction, which is quite understandable, but his contribution is really appreciable.

Friends will come from Afghanistan and Pakistan. From Hindustan, Dehlavi, Abidi and Qosimi will participate. They are deeply interested in Farsi-Tajiki literature and have been popularizing our sweet language. They have visited Tajikistan several times and participated in the commemorative celebrations of our illustrious ancestor like Jomi, Hafiz, Avicenna and Aini.

Guests come from other countries as well such as the US and Europe. I was in Paris where I met a young man who evinced keen interest in Farsi-Tajik literature. He told me that in the library of Sorbonne University and was running after the *Diwan* Kamal Khujandi, he could locate four manuscript copies of Kamal's *Diwan*. He studied all the four manuscripts besides the *diwans* published in Tajikistan, Moscow and Teheran. He had collated them and noted the discrepancies. He had located some unpublished *ghazals* and these he wants to use for participating in the commemorative function of Kamal in his native place. His name is Masud Mirshahi, who has founded a cultural association in Paris under the name of Rudaki Association. This is a cultural link between Farsi-Tajik speaking people of France and Tajikistan.

Another scholar Ahmad Hasan Hakkak Karimi from the US patronizes contemporary Tajik literature. He has translated the verses of Tajik poets into English and got them published. Such as poetry of Mumin Qanoat, Loiq and others.

Another friend Turaj Atabeki comes from Holland. He is interested in publishing the poems of our poets in the script of our ancestors (meaning in Arabic script). He promised to me that he would publish a selection from the verses of Gulrukhsar. He intends to publish a collection of the poems of the sweetest singing bulbul of Khujand, namely Farzaneh (I do not exaggerate) very soon. He may bring the draft copy with him when he comes to participate in the functions here. I must say that Farzaneh is our good luck. When I mention Farzaneh, Mahasti comes to my mind forthwith. If at one end of the line of the poets of Khujand stands Mahasti, Farzaneh stands at the other. The two make up the chain of celebrated poets of Khujand.

We are also expecting guests from other countries like Australia and Saudi Arabia. From Afghanistan, we shall be receiving Wasif Bakhtari, a well-known poet and a member of the World Tajik Association. As three events are inter-connected, most of our guests are almost common. When I was in Paris, an old friend from Afghanistan, Rawan Farhadi came to see me. He had heard about our program of organizing Kamal Khujandi commemoration function. He asked me if I would get him a letter of invitation. I said that I would certainly invite him. He said, "Please, tell the organizers that I would be making a presentation on Kamal's philosophy of love, the love that he considers the essence of life and the source of existence? I am a fan of his *ghazals* and I want to speak of my infatuation for the rose gardens of Khujand."

We are looking forward to the arrival of many more friends. I hope it does not remain just a show but a beginning of developing expertise on Kamal of Khujand. Permit me to say that we are debtors to the soul of Kamal. During our long past, we did not pay attention to Kamal. It would be in the fitness of things, and Kamal deserves that all Tajiks — from school going children to adults and seniors — remember by heart the verses (*ghazals*) of Kamal. We ought to introduce Kamal to ourselves and it in this conference we shall do that.

This May a seminar was organized by the Tajikistan Academy of Sciences in which some excellent and scholarly papers were presented by Tajik scholars to highlight various aspects of Kamal's poetry, philosophy and art. Now, as a sequel to that an international seminar will take place in Dushanbe but its inauguration and valedictory both in Khujand. This seminar will provide us the opportunity of listening to scholarly expositions of researchers from our country and those who come from abroad. We could publish these papers later on. This would be our spiritual treasure and Kamal's service to his people and his country, which is to enriching the spiritual aspect, which has assumed immense importance in contemporary times.

Spiritual spoliation leads to the spoliation of society, and corruption in society leads to corruption of the government. We ought to work towards spiritual ennoblement of our people. If you recollect, it is with this purpose after the celebration of the *Shahnameh* we announced that the next five years will continue to be dedicated to the *Shahname*. I would like that these celebrations continue. Likewise, I want that Kamal commemoration should continue even after the great commemorative function is over. People should read, understand and ruminate over the verses of Kamal, for they can cleanse their hearts of malice and hatred. Ferdowsi says:

Kineh az dilha birun kuned (sic)
Ba mehr o safa kishwar afzun kuned

Divest your hearts of malice
Bring plentiful to your country through love

Jami says:
Agar budi az jahl har sineh saf
Bar uftadi az khalq rasm-e khelaf

If all the hearts were cleansed ofobstinacy
The tradition of conflict among people would come to an end

If obstinacy and ignorance are shunned and conflict and estrangement abandoned, people can become friends. By coming closer to one another, their bonds of mutual support will get strengthened.

Q: Professor, Sir, in connection with Kamal commemoration, newspapers and journals published in our neighboring countries viz. Iran and Afghanistan have brought out articles on this great intellectual. We learn that articles have also been published in Uzbekistan to honor him. Could you please throw some light on this?

A: That is right. I returned from Tashkent only yesterday. I visited the office of the newspaper *Awaz-e Tajik*. Its chief editor, Shaukat Niyazi, a learned and accomplished person, is my old friend. He showed me the newspapers that had allotted a slot to the Kamal commemorative proceedings. A few articles have already been published. More articles will be published to introduce Kamal to Uzbek literati, especially the ethnic Tajiks of Uzbekistan. On behalf of the Chairman of Organizing Committee, I invited him to participate in our functions and report on the function and publish more writings to popularize the verses of Kamal.

I have already spoken about the two volumes published by Gulsurkhi. Numerous articles have been published in Iran and Afghanistan. In Europe too people know Kamal now and make him known to others in a better way.

The *diwan* of Kamal has been extensively copied; its copies can be found in many libraries of Hindustan and Pakistan. It is true that hitherto much less attention has been paid to Kamal. To be honest we, in Tajikistan, too, have shown indifference towards him. He stands in line with Hafiz, and their friendship should be a favorite subject for future research. Kamal has drawn from Hafiz, Hafiz, in turn, is reported to have said that when he read the *ghazals* of Kamal with the *radif* and *qafiya "goftam ba chashm"*, he was transported into a trance and tears rolled down his cheeks, particularly this verse:

Tashnehgan ra mujdeh-i az ma bebar/goftam ba chashm

Convey good news from me to the thirsty/ I said, surely I will

There is another poet we have neglected. I must confess that we have not done justice to our great intellectuals in a manner they deserve. I mean Nasir Bukharai. He was senior to Hafiz by seventeen years, and Hafiz has borrowed at least 35 *ghazals* of Nasir. This is also true about Kamal. The *diwan* of Nasir Bukharai is ready for publication. That is why we say that in the Kamal commemorative celebrations we should not only popularize the *ghazals* of Kamal but also those of Hafiz and Nasir Bukharai and other poets of the East. You may recollect what Abdur Rahman Jami, a fan of Kamal, has said:

Jami az lutf-e tarannum be ghazal ha-e Kamal
Andalibist khush ilham be chaman ha-e Khujand

Oh Jami, owing to the music in the *ghazals* of Kamal
He is a melodious bulbul in the gardens of Khujand

It is beautifully said. Likewise another great poet, the national pride of our Uzbek brethren, namely Alisher Navai Fani, was also fond of the *ghazals* of Kamal.

I would like to add one more point. As we are the compatriots of Kamal, we should try to understand the subtlety of his expression. We should understand the import of a book and inculcate in ourselves the habit of reading. We should induce our children to become readers. Unfortunately, book-reading is on a downward trend these days. This is an alarming scenario. We should popularize book reading. Our ancestors preserved books through thousands of years. During dark and calamitous days, they dumped books either in rivers or piled them in walls, and even carried them to their graves. Even in these difficult times, people preserve books in their private collections in their homes.

I would exhort one and all that today when we are afflicted with scarcity, we should not allow our fund of books to be taken out of our country for paltry sums. These works are our national wealth and international law prohibits taking out manuscripts from a country; it is tantamount to committing a crime.

When Professor Aini came to Dushanbe, an imposing house was built for him, which befitted his personality and stature. The story goes that he came in, went round the house and then came out and said, "This should be a treasure house for manuscripts and not as my residence. I can live in a one—room tenement." This is how our sage and savant laid the foundation of our manuscript library. He did a fine job and went his way. Today in Tajikistan we also erected a new structure there where more than five thousand rare manuscripts are preserved in the archives. A World Exhibition of rare books was organized in Paris. We carried some works from our archives for display in that exhibition and among these was a copy of the *Diwan* of Sa'adi transcribed during the lifetime of the great intellectual.

This is the reason why I exhort my countrymen to preserve handwritten manuscripts. These should be brought to the archives and preserved at one place so that they become a part of our national heritage. Our future generations will benefit from this. They will laud their ancestors and say that the fund was preserved despite the vicissitudes of time and vagaries of history.

Q: Respected Professor, we are thankful to you. I am confident that these three events, three impressive and splendid functions that are round the corner, will become an instrument for forging national solidarity, unity and mutual understanding among the people of Tajikistan.

A: Of course, I too nurse the same hopes. I want that each and every Tajik and each and every citizen of Tajikistan should realize his and her responsibility. I want them to speak each word and take each step with utmost caution. They should ask themselves how things can benefit them. Now you will have no hesitation in accepting that having passed through a history spread over several thousand years, there is nothing more sacred for us than that of preserving national solidarity and the government of the Tajiks. I yearn to arrive at this destination and I wish all of you health and happiness.

Thank you.

The End

My brother Osimi who is no more

By Prof. K.N. Pandita

Osimi is gone: I am left to mourn his death. Can there be an occasion sadder than this? To me he was not just Osimi the scholar, intellectual and friend: he was more than an elder brother to me. He was the epitome of the fabulous Central Asian civilization, a human monument embodying the eve and ebb of thousands of years of human history. Words cannot define his personality? It defies not only words but also comprehension. He was colossus of a human being, a Titan in true sense of the term.

In 1982, I was on the teaching staff of the Centre of Central Asian Studies at Kashmir University in India. Indian National Science Academy in New Delhi informed us that it was organizing three zone-wise seminars in India to celebrate one thousandth year of the great Central Asian philosopher and physician Abu Ali Sina (Avicenna). Our Centre was invited to host the northern zone seminar. As one who was entrusted with the organizing of seminars in the Centre, I accepted the assignment gladly and began to work on it.

Northern zone seminar was significant because most of the Indian experts on Central Asia came from northern universities. In Jawaharlal Nehru University, Central Asia formed part of its research institute called the School of International Studies. We had some eminent scholars from this and other universities and institutions.

Late Sheikh Muhammad Abdullah, the popular leader and Chief Minister of our State (Jammu & Kashmir) inaugurated the seminar. It was significant in the sense that he was the person who had conceived the idea of incepting the Centre of Central Asian Studies in Kashmir University. He had personally supervised the transfer of priceless artifacts from the State Toshakhana to the newly established Central Asian Museum. Amusingly, he personally supervised the transfer of this treasure.

Our seminar was much more successful than we had expected. The national press gave it wide coverage and throughout the country it was hailed as a big event.

Then, sometime in March/April 1983, the Indian National Science Academy organized the overarching seminar in which most eminent scholars who had participated in the three zonal seminars were invited to participate. I was also among the invitees. A number of outstanding scholars on Central Asian history and civilization were also invited. They came from the US, the UK, Germany, Iran, France, Turkey and many other countries. Professor Muhammad Osimi led the Central Asian delegation.

This was the first time when I met Osimi. He was very warm towards me and asked me many questions about the history and culture of Kashmir. I found him a soft-spoken man, with the light of an erudite in his eyes. He was physically a very handsome man, of moderate height, and pleasing features. A very close look as his physiognomy made me believe that it resembled that of Pandit Jawaharlal Nehru to a great extent. His fingers and limbs were chiselled, his gait regal, and his steps were confident. Osimi wore a broad smile, which showed he could be playful with children, serene with scholars, suave with diplomats and relaxed with colleagues. I had no difficulty in fathoming the depth and dimensions of his personality. Osimi was a superman.

We were together for three days in New Delhi. He presided over one of the sessions and delivered his speech in English. He had the perfect pronunciation and used the scientific idiom. But Osimi never spoke in English when he was with his compatriots or with those outsiders who could speak and understand Tajik.

In just three days, we became so close to each other as if we were old acquaintances. The curtain of formalities, inhibitions and reticence, all vanished. Osimi was drawn to me because in the course of exchanging pleasantries, I invariably took recourse to calling to mind a Tajik verse here and there. To me the test of culture is the impact of an apt Tajik verse on the listener. To my great surprise, I found I stood nowhere near Osimi in this faculty. This cemented our fraternal bonds which we both maintained till death snatched him from my hands.

From New Delhi, I sent a message home that our Centre in Kashmir should invite four or five foreign scholars who had come to participate in the New Delhi seminar. Osimi would lead this team. My proposal was conveyed to Sheikh Sahib, the Chief Minister in Srinagar, who immediately responded by fully agreeing to the proposal. I was directed to proceed immediately to Srinagar and make arrangements for the impending visit of the distinguished guests.

Three days later, the team of five foreign scholars led by Prof. Osimi landed at Srinagar airport. We were there to receive them. As they moved to the lounge for the special guests, a young officer of the State government stepped forward. Introducing himself to Osimi as the Director of the Protocol and Tourism, he announced that his (Osimi's) team was the guest of the State Government, and he was there representing the Chief Minister himself. I was taken aback for I had no information what the State government planned to do. In any case, my position was reduced to that of an interpreter, and perhaps this was a blessing in disguise. I came to know Osimi more and more. Each minute, I was to unfold new dimension of his personality.

The guests were lodged in the imposing government guesthouse by the side of river Jehlum, and within the looming shadows of the stately chinar trees. Osimi told me "Where is the schedule?" This one simple question made me realize that here was an administrator talking business. I got somewhat embarrassed because the Government and not the University was playing host. But I was relieved when the Director of Protocol told me that he would go by the schedule, which I had drawn earlier. There were a couple of state limousines at our disposal and the pilot from the traffic police.

Osimi agreed to the draft schedule, and immediately we began to go by it. It is difficult for me to recollect today, after about 16 years, the precise items we were to negotiate for the touring team. It included a function at the university, a visit to Gulmarg the hilly picnic spot, a private concert, reception by the Vice Chancellor and the Chief Minister, a visit to the manuscript library, a visit to downtown Srinagar and the shopping centre. I can recollect a couple of incidents pertaining to this programme.

In the university, there was a gathering of about two hundred persons, students and members of teaching staff. I introduced the guests briefly. In his welcome speech, the Vice Chancellor, who was chairing the function, first read out the message from the Chief Minister. It was all courtesy, warmth and good wishes.

The Vice Chancellor himself made a speech and spoke of our ancient ties with Central Asia. Then Osimi spoke for nearly half an hour. He traced the story of our historical links with Central Asia often shifting to cultural links of lasting nature. The audience cheered him every five minutes for he spoke in Tajik and I translated it into English for the audience. His extempore speech showed how deeply knowledgeable he was about the history, geography, culture, economy, geopolitics, and above all the history of fraternal relations among the Asians of this region. Towards the end of his speech, he said to the audience, *"Shuma taj-e—sar-e ma hasted"* meaning you are a crown on our head. I did not translate it. He repeated it thrice and thrice I declined to translate it. The audience did not sense it and the meeting came to a close. Outside the auditorium, he furiously asked me why did not I translate that particular sentence when he had desired it not once but thrice. I politely said," Your Excellency, you the Central Asians are the crown on our head. Our ancestors (*nayakan*) came all the way from Central Asia to this land thousands of years ago. We can't be the crown on your head." Osimi hugged me hard, planted a kiss on my cheeks and said, *"azeez-e ma hasted"* you are dear to us.

We were meandering along the dense Gulmarg forest road to reach the top of the e heights and enjoy the panoramic view of the Valley and the Himalayas. Along the road, lush green and beautiful bushes looked like gazelles lining the path. I whispered into Osimi's ear:

hameh ahuwan-e—sahra sar-i khud nihadeh bar kaf
be khayal-e an kih ruzi be shikar khwahi amad

He was thrilled and looked straight into my eyes saying, "Ah me! This remote corner of the world; this dense forest; this Tajik verse and its vivid background! Is there any greater proof than this of our common cultural heritage? This was Osimi, the poet, the idealist, the romanticist, the historian and the man with limitless vision.

On reaching the top of Gulmarg Mountain, we were ushered into the guesthouse, which, during the days of the Maharaja of Kashmir, was his exclusive preserve. The day was sunny and bright and from the balcony, we looked in distant north to see with naked eye the second highest peak of the Himalayas called Kanchinjunga or K 2. It was clad in shimmering white snow, majestic and imposing. I remember Osimi said this was a moment for him, which he would never forget. I could see a child's glee on his face and innocent light in his eyes. He was inexplicably overjoyed. The lunch served in that historic lodge was equally memorable. As we motored down the meandering road, we saw a sprinkling of fresh snow on the ground. May be it had fallen the previous night. I do not know how, but a folk verse very common among us Kashmiris came to my lips and I did not hesitate to whisper it into the ears of Osimi. I said:

Barf-e now aftad, sad mubarak bad, anchih wada kardi zood bayad dad.

I explained that on the occasion of the first snowfall of the year, children rising early in the morning find the white sheet spread out on the ground and take a flake in their hand and offer it to their elders as a gift. If it is received inadvertently, the child speaks out the verse, and, of course, he must receive a coin. Osimi was amazed that this was precisely the folklore tradition in Tajikistan during the days of his childhood. And then in a lighter vein said, "Yes I will give you a gift of a visit to Tajikistan." The same year in summer, he invited me to Dushanbe and I spent more than a memorable month with my Tajik friends.

The third incident was that of a local Kashmiri singer who entertained us with some Tajik *ghazals* late at night in the guesthouse. He was playing on the *tar,* one—string musical instrument. At the height of singing, he got ecstatic, and in that state of ecstasy began dancing with the instrument in his hand. It was Amir Khusrav's this ghazal:

kafir-e ishqam musalmani mara dar kar nest
har rag-e man tar gashteh hajat-e zunnar nest

I noticed that Osimi was gradually turning red in his cheeks and pounding his foot on the floor. Lo and behold! He suddenly rose on his feet, moved towards the ecstatic singer, took his hand and began dancing in equal ecstasy. He forgot himself; he forgot he was the President of Tajik Academy of Sciences, an important person in the Soviet Union, a state guest and a great scholar. He was Osimi, the pure and innocent Osimi, the child of nature, and the lover of beauty, poetry, music and dance, the truest representative of the "freemen" (Aer) of historic Central Asia. This then was another dimension of Osimi's personality — Osimi, my friend, brother and guide, whose obituary I am called upon to write. What a tragedy and what an irony?

On his invitation (as the Chairman of Tajik Academy of Sciences), I proceeded to Dushanbe on September 7, 1983 (the same year). In those days, we had to take the Delhi-Moscow-Dushanbe flight. At Moscow, a representative of the Soviet Academy of Sciences received me. I wondered how she could locate me in that huge crowd at Sheremetayevo airport. It was simple, the intelligent female told me. "I found you were the only person without an overcoat. Indians do not know of an overcoat because they never have a winter." As we drove to the Soviet Academy guesthouse, she extended her hand asking me to look at the lines and tell her what was there in her destiny. Was she a sad, deprived or a betrayed woman? Such is the frailty of human beings. It speaks of what common Russians think of us, the Indians — foretellers, soothsayers, magicians and all that. Unfortunate for her, I was none of this stuff.

In the Guest House in Moscow, a message from Osimi was delivered to me saying that I could stay in Moscow for three or four days for sight-seeing and meeting with academics. A young Muscovite was put in charge of me who told me that I was to get the amount of one month's allowance from Moscow itself under instructions from Dushanbe. For three or four days, he conducted me in Moscow and I saw a lot of that great and historic city including the Kremlin. Twice during those four days of stay in Moscow, did Osimi call me on phone and enquire about my welfare saying if I wanted to stay in Moscow for a few days more, I could without any difficulty. I told him that I would like to be in the warm climate of Dushanbe as early as possible. Next day, I found myself boarding the plane for Dushanbe. This gave me an idea how much care Osimi was taking of me. Indeed he was inquiring from his contacts every night about my welfare and comfort. This was Osimi, the foremost in preserving of the great tradition of warm hospitality of the Tajiks. That tradition is traceable in the *Shahnameh* of Ferdowsi.

Abdullah Jan Ghaffarov, now no more in this world, received me at Dushanbe airport and brought me to Hotel Tajikistan. The same evening Osimi gave me a call and welcomed me to Dushanbe hoping that I would certainly enjoy my trip to Tajikistan. Next morning, Abdullah Jan and Prof. Ahrar Mukhtarov came to see me in the hotel, and drew up the programme for the day. I took to Dushanbe and its people as a fish takes to water. Everything looked familiar to me. I felt I was a part of everything around me. Then came

71

a call from Osimi. His driver was to arrive shortly and drive me to his place. This was the first of several dinners I had with him in his house. But I must describe it in some detail.

In the large dining room, I found about a dozen or more people seated around the dining table. It was laden with fruits of many varieties, ripe grapes, pomegranates, and apples, apricots, and etc. all in heaps. Immense chinaware was spread out on the table and the eatables began to make round after round. At the top of the table sat Madam Osimi with a woman guest from Afghanistan. Among the guests, there was Sher Ali, a minister in Afghanistan. Among other notable persons were Madam Golrukhsar, the Tajik poetess and Jura Beg, the famous Tajik singer. But most notable were two or three gaunt persons who were introduced to me as Pamirians and relatives of Osimi family. Perhaps they were holding some official positions.

As the dinner proceeded, Osimi beckoned to Jura Beg who took his *tar* and sang a beautiful *ghazal* of Hafiz of Shiraz. Everybody enjoyed the great singer at the best of his performance. The interludes were filled with jokes, stories, verses, anecdotes, lampoons and titbits. Osimi beckoned to Madam Golrukhsar who obliged and recited a couple of her recently composed verses. These spoke about maternal affection. Madam Osimi took the floor and recited the famous verses of the Iranian poet Iraj Mirza in this context beginning :

"goyand mara chu zad madar/ pistan be dahan giriftan amokht"

The room resounded with cheers. Another Tajik poetess sitting by the side of Madam Golrukhsar also recited her two poems, which were followed by another orgy of *ghazal* recitation by Jura Beg. As the atmosphere warmed up and the guests responded by word and action, one by one they rose from their seats and began dancing on sidelines. More warmth was injected into the carnival. Then Osimi stowed the chairs and sofa to another room and made space for the guests to indulge in revelry, dancing, singing and beating their feet and hands. As the merrymaking proceeded, there dashed into the room a small child of barely four years, Osimi's grandchild. He took it in his lap and then began dancing with us asking the child to lift its hands. The party, eating, drinking, singing, music, dancing and chatting continued till two hours past midnight. Everybody was happy and in the finest of spirits. Osimi recounted episode after episode of his life. I cannot forget how in most eloquent words he had introduced me to the guests and how much regard they had for India and Indian civilization. He said he was happy that a person who embodied the best of Tajik and Indian culture was his guest that night. I felt embarrassed but he meant it. He asked me to recite verses and I obliged producing a variety of Tajik-Persian verses spanning a long period of Iranian history. When the toast was proposed, everybody made an impressive speech but the Afghan minister made a lengthy harangue, which, as I remember, reflected great concern for Tajik-Afghan friendship. And I on my turn spoke just three sentences and sat down. Osimi said brevity is the soul of wit.

Osimi escorted me to his car to send me back to my hotel. In a whisper he said, "We the Tajik are like that. I did this all to honour you. But tell me was it anyway better than the event we had in Srinagar one night?" I said there was no comparison. Tajik hospitality and finesse are unparalleled. With a hug and a kiss, he bade me good bye, but warned me that there was a very heavy schedule waiting for me. This then was my late friend and brother Osimi, a man of wide ranging tastes; poetry, music, recitation, table talk, emotion, taste for good food, hospitality, dignity, respect and sincerity. Madam Osimi too had accompanied her husband to see me off and she told me that her house was as good as my own house. There was simplicity and dignity and these were the hallmark of Osimi's life and character.

When late Abdullah Jan and I returned after a ten days-tour of Central Asia, which took us to Tashkent, Penjikent, Samarkand and Bokhara, Osimi asked him whether we had visited Leninabad. He was simply dismayed to learn from Abdullah Jan we had not. He talked to me warmly about Khujand and asked me which of the famous poets of Khujand did I know. Obviously Kamal was the answer and he asked me to recite any verse from Kamal. I obliged:

chun barkanam dil az tu wa bardaram az tu mehr
an mehr bar kih afganam an dil kuja baram

Believe me Osimi could not contain himself. He was agog with joy. Raising both hands he exclaimed, "I am proud of you." Then for the first time he said to me, "Professor Pandita, you are our cultural ambassador in India."

Osimi cared for the prestige and honour of his people and his country. It was as great an honour to me as to India or Tajikistan. I bowed my head in thanks and he rose from his chair to embrace me. Wasn't Osimi more than a brother? Wasn't he a great son of the soil? Indeed, Osimi, the martyr ennobled his motherland with his blood in letter and in spirit.

Abdullah Jan told me that we were to meet with Osimi in his office in the Academy of Sciences. His private secretary, Madam Natasha ushered us in. Osimi had called in a few senior professors to be introduced to me. He talked briefly of the Academy of Sciences and quickly shifted to culture, history, civilization, society and Indo-Tajik relations. He was proud to say that he enjoyed the respect from Indians, their senior academics and officials. That was very true as I came to know of it later on. Osimi said that we all had to do a lot to strengthen our relations. Then addressing the professors gathered there he said that India had kept the light burning and that Prof. Pandita was the proof. He presented to me a few books and asked Abdullah Jan about our programme during next few days. It revealed that he was keeping himself fully aware of my programmes and business. When the bell rang, Natasha, the private secretary, led us out. It was the same Natasha who rang me up from Moscow last year to break the tragic news that Osimi was no more in this world. She said it was her personal loss. But to me it was a tragedy. It was a severe blow to the entire Tajik nation and friends of Tajikistan.

My visit to Tajikistan was nearing its end. I went to see Osimi in his house. He had already been informed. It was a one to one meeting. He was exceptionally cordial, warm and kind. He said," *Aya in musafarat be shuma* ma'q*ul amad*?" Was this visit to your liking? Having done so much for me, having given me so much of love and affection, Osimi was still more magnanimous as to ask me whether my visit was of my liking. Madam Osimi brought tea, fruits, and a heap of eatables. The couple sat with me for more than an hour talking of many things. The picture of that meeting is vivid before my eyes. Both of them told me repeatedly that it was not my last visit, and that Tajikistan would call me again and again. These words were prophetic. In September 1999, I was on my sixth visit to Tajikistan.

In 1986, Indian Council of Cultural Relations organized in collaboration with the Government of India, the second Asian conference in New Delhi. It was one of the biggest conferences I have ever attended.

Delegates from more than 80 Asian countries were invited. There were scores of observers from the western countries and the full battery of international media. The delegates were lodged in five-star hotels in New Delhi. Fortunately Osimi and I were putting up in the same hotel (Ashoka). This gave me an opportunity of seeing more of Osimi. We used to meet at breakfast and talk on a variety of subjects. He was very happy with the reception given to a small team of distinguished foreign guests including Osimi, by the then Prime Minister, Rajiv Gandhi.

I do not exactly remember the names of other scholars from Central Asia who had accompanied Osimi to the conference. But I was present among the audience when he made his formal presentation, which was in English. Unfortunately, I have misplaced the copy of the text but I distinctly remember that his speech reflected the wide range of his thought and approach. He talked in global and universal terms rising far above others in vision, analysis and assessment. Here I found Osimi the statesman, the diplomat and the scholar. The words were extremely well chosen and balanced and the sentences revealed the conviction of the man. He had grace, poise and warmth. Though he represented the Soviet Union in his capacity as the leader of the delegation, yet Osimi spoke and thought like an Asian and a well—wisher of the Asian people, transcending territorial limits of countries and nations. I thought he was the most respected delegate to the conference.

This seminar revealed tome that Osimi was very friendly to late Mr. P.N. Haksar, once the principal secretary to Indira Gandhi. The other Indian dignitary with whom he had very cordial relations was Prof. Nurul Hasan, once Chairman CSIR and later on Governor of West Bengal.

In 1991-92, New Delhi was the venue for a meeting of the organizing committee of UNESCO's project on the History of Central Asia. The UNESCO published the *Central Asian Journal* and Osimi had given them my name and address to be put on their mailing list. It was a journal of very high research standard with contributions from some of the most brilliant scholars of Soviet Union. Osimi had already recommended my name for inclusion among the observers in the said meeting. The other distinguished foreign scholar present in this meeting was Professor Dani, the well-known Pakistani epigraphist and archaeologist. The agenda for this meeting was drafting of the contents for various chapters of the third volume of the History of Central Asia. This volume was to deal with the mediaeval and later mediaeval times. Therefore, Indian and foreign experts in the field were invited to discuss issues. Osimi and Professor Nurul Hasan chaired the meeting alternatively.

Scholars usually make a huge fuss on such occasions. This meeting was not an exception. But Osimi handled situations with deftness, clarity and exactitude. He would make interventions, short, to the point and illuminating. Everybody wondered how much depth and width of knowledge this man had that he could address even the subtle points raised by speakers. This was Osimi, the astute scholar, historian and commentator.

Osimi was lodged in India International Centre, New Delhi. He told me in private that he wanted to stay in Delhi for a few days more and then go to Calcutta on the invitation of Governor Nurul Hasan. We arranged his extended stay immediately. Again he called me and asked me to tie up his programme when he returned from Calcutta. He was scheduled to fly to Islamabad from Bombay. I took up the matter with the ICCR who extended full cooperation and assured me that he would be taken care of when he came back from Calcutta.

When I conveyed to him at India International Centre that all arrangements were made, I found that he had changed his mind and was no more willing to go to Calcutta. Instead he wanted to spend a few days in Delhi to wait for the flight to Islamabad. I immediately assured him that if he wanted to change his schedule, there was no difficulty. He seemed to be happy and then told me to speak to Governor Nurul Hasan that he had changed his programme.

I did not disclose to Nurul Hasan that in case Osimi decided to stay back in New Delhi, ICCR would take care of him. I tried to assure him of having made full arrangements but he had reservations. The truth was that Nurul Hasan certainly wanted Osimi to come to Calcutta as the guest of the Governor and enjoy a couple of days of his company. Who would not want to be with Osimi even if it was just an hour or two? He was a fine conversationalist and had a large fund of anecdotes and real stories to tell. I left for Jammu but kept the track of things, and came to know that Osimi had returned to Delhi after staying in Calcutta for about a week and had proceeded to Pakistan.

Here I may go back to the winter of 1983-84. After my return from my first visit to Tajikistan in September—October 1983, I decided to spend two and a half months of winter vacation with my daughter's family who were then in Trivandrum in Kerala (South India). The reason was that I wanted real seclusion to compile from my notes an account of my travel to Tajikistan. Fortunately I seized the opportunity. I wrote to Osimi to send me his photograph because I wanted to write the travelogue and dedicate it to him. After all he was the moving spirit behind my first travel to Tajikistan. Osimi quickly sent me a photograph showing him in his younger days in his personal library. It was an excellent photograph in black and white and I preserved it carefully.

The travelogue under the title *My Tajik Friends* was printed and published in Delhi perhaps in spring 1984. I sent its copies to some of my close friends in Tajikistan, Osimi being the first one on the list. Its receipt was acknowledged with thanks. Later on I came to know that everybody in Tajikistan who read the travelogue liked it.

In autumn 1987, I was again in Dushanbe for about a month. Again Osimi invited me to his house for dinner. But this time, we were only the family members sitting around the dining table. In a sense, this get together was much more memorable for me. Osimi talked on a very important subject and talked like a university professor explaining and exposing the subject in full and authenticated detail. He talked about the contribution of Russians in the socio-economic transformation of Central Asia under Soviet power. He talked about the great and incredible sacrifices made by the Russians during the World War II. It seemed as if I was screening a documentary. Osimi told of his personal experiences as a soldier on the war front. He said once in extremely cold weather when everything was frozen, he along with other soldiers held a bunker and kept constant vigil for three days and nights without food to eat. On the night of the third day, the platoon commander, a Russian, came to the bunker and some food was also brought but it was no more than a couple of morsels. The platoon commander himself had been without food for three days. As the few pieces of black bread were distributed, the commander passed on his share to us and told us that each one of us could take two hours rest by turn and he would himself replace the retiring soldier on duty. In this way, the platoon commander kept vigil for the whole night with sub zero temperature and with empty stomach. Then Osimi added this sentence. *"Rus ha in taur hastand."* (Such are the Russians). I shall never forget the lengthy details in which he told me the incredible contribution of the Russians in transforming life, economy and standard of living in Central Asia under Soviet power. He had himself been through the entire process and a part of it. He said this subject needed to be entrusted to eminent researchers so that in the course of history, we do not lose sight of the sacrifices they made for us. It will be nothing short of irony if at any time in future, Central Asians neglect or underestimate the contribution of the Russians in developing the vast region. The infrastructure that we see today in Central Asia is in itself the evidence of what is stated here. Osimi particularly referred to the changes brought about in far off villages and mountainous areas of Tajikistan by the Soviet system notwithstanding the fact that much more remains to be done still. Thus he gave a proof of his honest scholarship by recognizing the facts of history. This was Osimi, a man above prejudices, a man above many human weaknesses and always taking cosmopolitan view of things. Osimi was a citizen of the world in true sense of the term never confining only to his compatriots. He was highly conscious of his cultural heritage but he was appreciative of other peoples and societies with their colourful history and culture.

Osimi told me that he had decided that my travelogue is translated into Russian.

A year later, Osimi informed me that my travelogue had been translated into Russian and several thousand copies were published and distributed in Dushanbe. A couple of copies of Russian translation were mailed to me. He told me that I would be getting the royalty from sale proceeds, which, however, I declined to accept.

In October 1987, I made a brief trip to Moscow, Leningrad, Tashkent and Dushanbe. This was part of the Sovietland Nehru Award given to me for my small service to the strengthening of Indo-Tajik cultural relations. The travelogue had become the catalyst for this award. During this visit, I was in Dushanbe for only three days. I missed the opportunity of meeting him once more as he was away in France on official business.

After 1990, events took a different turn in the Soviet Union. Perestroika and Glasnost were in the air and beneath all that was the lurking fear, which proved a reality. Soviet Union's Afghan policy was disastrous. Bad and disturbing news was coming in day in and day out. When you stand at a distance from a mountain, you can comprehend its height. So did we, sitting at a distance, comprehending the magnitude of the turn of history in that region? Tajikistan was close to the scene of turmoil; so was Kashmir.

I made it my routine to listen regularly to news and commentaries from Radio Tajikistan. Out of curiosity, I also continued listening to Tajik programmes of Radio Liberty. I would ponder over the unfolding of horrendous events from the womb of time. I shuddered, and the history of the entire ancient geographical region from Avestic Haitamandu (Helmand) river to the Turanian lands of Zarafshan valley in the north turned its pages before my eyes one after another. What had the future in store for it was the nagging question.

I cared for my Tajik friends, for all the Tajiks and for all the Central Asians. For a pretty long time, there was no news of Osimi or of others whom I knew so well in Tajikistan. Occasionally, I would pay a visit to Delhi and meet some of my colleagues and friends in Jawaharlal University who had travelled either to Tashkent or Moscow or to Alma Ata (now Almaty), and some of them would tell me that they had heard about Osimi in Dushanbe. This would relieve me of my anxiety. Some people began coming from Dushanbe to Delhi and I met a few of them. I came to know that Osimi had relinquished the office of President of Tajik Academy. He was now heading the cultural organization called *Paywand*.

In 1992, (if I remember well), Osimi came to New Delhi to attend a seminar. The organizers also invited me. I met him in his hotel room (India International Centre) but apparently Osimi was not in his usual frame of mind. He appeared a disturbed man. I could understand what was there in his mind and there was no need to touch on those matters. He gave me a letter of invitation to participate in the first convention of international forum of Tajik people and Friends in Dushanbe from September 9 to 16, 1992. It was being organized under the aegis of Paywand of which he was the Chairman. Along with this he gave me a letter for the Russian Embassy in New Delhi requesting to issue me a visa. I did not see more of Osimi this time because he himself was vague about his programme. I suspect he did not want to be probed about it and I did not make even a single inquiry.

But Osimi's invitation to me proved futile because no organization in India was prepared to finance my visit, at least the return airfare. But what I did was a very unique thing. I kept complete and hour-by-hour and event-by-event track of the functions, seminars and meetings held in Dushanbe for three stipulated days. My radio wavelength remained fixed on Dushanbe station and I recorded the entire proceedings. Later on, I made a comprehensive note out of it and sent it to the Indian Council of Cultural Relations more out of anger than anything else. Conspicuously, I had recorded the welcome and other speeches of Osimi, which gave me great solace and satisfaction that my dear friend had not been exhausted by the sad events that had overtaken Tajikistan in the aftermath of independence. I was overjoyed to hear his voice. Osimi generally spoke in broken sentences. But he was extraordinarily careful with the selection of words and phrases. I could create his image on the canvas of my mind as he spoke with halting poise.

With the assistance of the Indian Council of Cultural Relations, I was again in Dushanbe in September 1995 on a two week visit. Dushanbe was a different place now. The main part of the town betrayed clear and unmistakable signs of destruction and devastation. The vehicular traffic was off the road for there was no fuel and the public transport system had totally broken down. Shanties built of mud walls and roofed with scrap stood along the once prestigious avenues. Not a single newspaper was published; not a single sheet of white paper was available to write a letter on. In the Hotel Tajikistan, there was absolutely nothing to eat. Electric and water supply system had broken down except for a few specific places. Roads broken and desolate, houses presenting a sad and sickening view, parks crying for upkeep, water fountains all dry—this was the scene. At every nook and corner, droves of young men squatted on the road looking a passer—by with poignant curiosity. Many friends I knew had left the town and gone to their respective villages to eke out a miserable living because the life in city was not worth anything. The street leading from bazaar to Hotel Tajikistan from the north was a long bed of dust and dirt. In pre-revolution days, it was so neat and tidy that I often used to take it for a morning walk. The newly built two-storey teahouse on Lenin Street (now Rudaki Street) had been closed and other restaurants wore a deserted look. People wore dusty shoes and clad themselves in tatters. I shudder when I bring back to mind the desolate picture of Dushanbe in 1995. I had seen Dushanbe a number of times in the past: it was vibrant and full of life. People moved around in complete safety and security. The huge park in front of Hotel Tajikistan used to hum with life; retired soldiers playing chess or volleyball. Young couples enjoying hot appetizing *osh*, dancing and singing to the tune of the musicians throbbing and vitalizing the onlookers. Everything had gone and the silence and desolation of the graveyard prevailed. However, in the bazaar, fresh fruits came in abundance as usual but the customers thronging the place were not the same, which I was used to see. Truly the government was non-functional.

My friend, Professor Ahrar Mukhtaraov took me to the place where the office of Paywand was situated. We had a meeting with Osimi. He welcomed me as usual with warmth. I found he had overcome the despondency of previous year. He did not talk of the tragic events that had befallen Tajikistan in previous years but concentrated on *Paywand*. I can recall he had some plans for making Paywand a strong and vibrant organization. The question was of funds. Nevertheless, a clear-headed man, as he was, he had definite plans for its development. He offered us fruits, tea and usual sprinkling of jokes and told me that I had to have dinner with him one of those days. I can say with confidence that the history of recent one decade had made its impression on him and I thought he wanted to either write it down or recount it to a confident person. His eyes showed that he wanted to speak. May be had I time at my disposal he would have spoken to me. I had none and I regret why I failed to seize the opportunity. How on earth could I know that this moving treasure would be snatched from our hands by fate?

A message came to me that Osimi would like me to attend the marriage ceremony of a friend of his. It was Sunday and a car carried me to the place where the function was held. It was across the bridge on the right side in a spacious courtyard. I have had lots of such invitations whenever I am in Dushanbe. As such, I knew the way Tajiks enjoyed it. Osimi had already arrived and was sitting at the head of a table around which sat many known and important persons. He introduced me to them one by one repeating that here was Tajikistan's most affectionate Indian friend. He gave me a seat next to himself. The huge eating spree began as usual with speeches, recitations, singing and dancing. As the white liquid made its effect on guests, the warmth turned onto the function. The setting sun spread its crimson rays on the tables and colourful dresses of beautiful Tajik women who danced to their hearts' content.

Here I shall recount two sentences, which Osimi and myself exchanged between us on the spur of the moment. There was some casual reference to the Afghan fighting and the rising crescendo of Taliban in that country. Osimi turned towards me and said," What is your opinion about the situation developing in Afghanistan, the rise of Taliban and its impact?" I said, "If Taliban succeed in their mission in Afghanistan, you, dear Osimi, will not find gala functions like this anymore in your country." He was so much amused with the remark that he threw up his hands and asked those around to listen what "the Indian friend had to say." He repeated my words several times and in particular to famous Tajik poet Laiq Sherali, who sat next to Osimi.

Then he put his arm round mine and said that I must address the gathering. I knew it is the custom with Tajiks that a guest is to say a few sentences of thanks to the organizers and blessings to the couple. He took me by arm and slowly walked across the courtyard to the stand behind which the mike had been placed for the speakers. He slowly whispered into my ear that I should say a few words in appreciation of the poetry of Laiq Sherali, the most outstanding contemporary poet of Tajikistan. He said that I could announce a reception in honour of this poet if he chose to pay a visit to India. In fact, as I came to know later on Osimi was inclined to send a group of Tajik artists to India on a visit to strengthen Indo-Tajik cultural relations.

As already said, Osimi was gifted with a multi-dimensional personality. He was clear-headed, subtle, a man of few words (except when in lighter mood), one who believed in action. There was a majestic dignity in his words and movement, a steady and solid personality seeing whom one would say, "This is the Man."

He beckoned to someone to carry me back to Hotel Tajikistan. I thanked everybody. Osimi hugged me and kissed me on the cheek. Then we shook hands and I left. I cast a parting glance at Osimi. Alas! I did not know this would be the last sight of Osimi for me. I motored away in the darkness of the night. Darkness did prevail. I had seen Osimi for the last time, and the darkness continues to engulf my mind.

In September 1999, three years after I had seen Osimi for the last time, I found myself again in Dushanbe to participate in the 1100th anniversary of Samanid state. The President of Tajikistan had invited me. There could be no bigger an honour for an ordinary man like myself. The first glimpse of Dushanbe brought me immense joy. It was not the Dushanbe of 1996. Dushanbe wore a festive look. The roads were again asphalted, traffic was brisk along the streets, electricity and water supply were fully resumed, youth no more squatted in groups on the roadside, shanties had been removed, and the city looked attractive. Civic life had returned to the strife-torn town. Nothing could make me happier.

But then I stood on the footpath and thought of Osimi, his family, his house and the whole story of my association with him. I asked my caretakers to take me to Osimi's house. They said that after the tragedy had happened, the family moved to their native Khujand. I was pained and sad that I could not meet Madam Osimi or the children to convey my condolence in person. I had, of course written a condolence letter immediately after the tragedy took place but I was not sure whether it had reached them. What could I do now? Somebody told me that Osimi's brother was in the town and I forthwith told my hosts to get me into touch with him. But no success was visible. Our organizers said they might take a group on a short excursion to Khujand. I insisted that I be included in that group. But even that too did not materialize. Was I doomed to go back to India with a mind bandaged in unrelieved sadness? Out on the street, I kept on gazing at every neatly dressed person of middling age to assure myself it was or was not Osimi. It was not, and I would relapse into a state of despondency. How could I believe I was in Dushanbe and Osimi was not to be seen and not to be met with anymore? I craved to see the house he lived in and we met in so many times. I craved to see the chair he sat in when he told me for two hours the long story of the service of Russians to Central Asians in their task of development. I was engulfed by deep sadness.

But then happened a strange thing, which assured me that there was not only worldly connection between Osimi and me and his family, but some spiritual relation too. A loud knock at the door of my room in Hotel Avesta one afternoon brought me to the presence of a dear person, Gavhar, Osimi's daughter was standing before me. Could I believe my eyes? Was wide-awake or was I dreaming?

Gavhar sat in the chair. I wanted to cry loud, very loud. I wanted to kiss her hands in whose veins the blood of my dear friend Osimi flows. I looked intently at her face; I saw in it eloquent contours of Osimi's nose, chin and voice. Now Gavhar was not only Osimi's daughter, she was as good as my own daughter. I could not control myself, and I cried and Gavhar cried and we both cried. "What wrong had Osimi done to whomsoever?" I kept on asking myself. With difficulty, we overcame the sentiment of grief and loss. Gavhar told me that she had been looking for me for last two days. She wanted my impressions about Osimi. She came back next day at the appointed time and told me to extend my stay and visit Khujend.

Honestly, I was eager to see the family, which is now my own family, and console them. But I had to go by the wishes of the organizers.

Thus, left with not many days of life as I am, my heart goes to the children of my friend in Khujand. They are as good as my own children, part of my life. Who knows that we descended from the same ancestors who were one another's kith and kin before they migrated from Central Asia to northern India, thousands of years ago? The blood speaks. So do I speak to Osimi's children, and they speak tome, the descendents of our common ancestors.

The End

M. Osimi - President of the Academy of Sciences of Tajikistan. Dushanbe, 1980

Payvand guests visit the memorial of Sadriddin Ayni in Dushanbe, 1992.

The meeting of the International Scientific Committee of UNESCO in Dushanbe, 1990.

Conducting a meeting of the Tajik Language Terminology Committee (from right to left M.Osimi, A.Maniyozov and other members) Dushanbe. 1990's

Celebration of Hafiz, Dushanbe 1971.

The Celebration of 100th anniversary of Sadriddin Ayni, Dushanbe 1978.

Monument of Firdausi erected during the Forum of the Tajiks in Dushanbe, September 1992.

M. Osimi and Mirzo Tursun-Zade, Dushanbe,1970's

Official visit in India. Delhi,1981

Opening ceremony of the Academy of Sciences of Afghanistan. Kabul, 1980

Handing Avicenna prize to one of the Tajik selectionists. 1970's

UNESCO,Paris 1977

At the Academy of Sciences of Tajikistan with Prof.Ahmad Hasan
Dani and Prof.Miroshnikov. Dushanbe, 1993

Professor Osimi and Professor Ahmad Hasan Dani, Dushanbe 1993.

M. Osimi and K.Pandita, Lahor,1980

The center of Pakistan and Iran cultures, Islamabad, 1993

The center of Pakistan and Iran cultures, Islamabad ,1993
From left to right: Sahbani,Sultan-zade, Osimi, Yuldashev, Dani, Khairullaev, Tashiri

Speech at the 74th inter-Parliamentary Congress in Ottawa, 1985

At the conference devoted to the 100th anniversary of Jawaharlal Nehru.
Prof. Osimi and Prof. Pandita, Delhi. October, 1989

M.Osimi and Uktam Kholiknazarov at the Payvand office, Dushanbe 1992.

M. Osimi and Dr. Karimi Hakkok, Seattle, United States 1994.

Meeting with the Yakubian family, New York, United States 1992.

Members of Payvand at the Academy of Sciences of Tajikistan, Dushanbe 1995.

M.Osimi and Akbar Tursun (on the right) with Abulkasim Lahuti's family.

From left to right: R.Yusufbekov, Hossein Daneshpour, Monand Osimi, Charlotta, Masoudi Sepand, Osimi's grandaughter Nargis, Askar Hakim, Firuza and Sarvar Osimi (Osimi's daughters) in the Osimi's house, Dushanbe 1994.

From left to right Siyavush Somi, Prof.Kashinat Pandita, Hossein Daneshpour: meeting in the memory of M.Osimi. Denver, United States 2005.

From left to right: Hossein Daneshpour, Masoud Mirshahi, Mustafo Osimi(Osimi's son), USA 2001.

M. Osimi in 1941

Medals from WWII, Dushanbe 1985.

Muhammad and Monand Osimi, Dushan be 1982.

Osimi's family, Dushanbe 1988.

M.Osimi with grandchildren: (from left to right) Parviz, Shahnoz, Nigora,
Jaffar, Dilovar, Nargis, Daler, Ravhsan, Dushanbe 1982.

The last spring of Muhammad Osimi. Dushanbe, March 1996

Printed in the United States
by Baker & Taylor Publisher Services